The Crocodile File

Dan Colman

Arthur Barker Limited · London

A subsidiary of Weidenfeld (Publishers) Limited

Published in Great Britain by
Arthur Barker Limited
91 Clapham High Street
London SW4 7TA

ISBN 0 213 16940 1 .

Typesetting by Ampersand Communication Limited, London

Printed in Great Britain by
Butler & Tanner, Frome and London

Introduction

On a misty afternoon in the autumn of 1937, I and a party of close friends set out on a fishing expedition up the Surrey Commercial Canal between Bermondsey and Peckham Rye.

Foolhardily, whilst proudly examining my catch in a jam-jar, I ventured perilously close to the treacherous slimy edge of the bank and, losing my footing, plunged headlong into the murky waters. Desperately I tried to swim but soon realised I had not yet learned how to. My pitifully improvised strokes took me backwards in the opposite direction from my friends and the security of the bank.

I sunk once, and then twice. I vividly recall opening my eyes and being struck by the menacing thick browny, grey-green colour of the water. I then distinctly remember going down for the third time and thinking at the time of sinking 'THE THIRD TIME DOWN — IS THE TIME YOU DROWN'. I closed my eyes stoically and prepared myself for eternity. The next thing I remember was a vice-like grip around my waist. My god, I thought. A crocodile!!!

I was then dragged upwards, which even as a six-year-old I thought a bit odd. I had always imagined crocodiles dragged their prey downwards. I remember thinking perhaps he hadn't learned to swim either.

As I broke through the surface of the water I looked up and saw a red striped tie and a face wearing glasses.

The next thing I remember was standing naked in front of a glowing kitchen range, being rubbed down, and drinking a cup of steaming sweet cocoa. I was in a small cosy kitchen of one of the little houses that backed on to the canal.

My life had been saved by a crocodile wearing a striped tie and spectacles.

In truth, I must admit to the reader that this is the one and only real encounter I have ever had with a crocodile in my entire life, and that what follows in this book is pure fiction.

Dan Colman

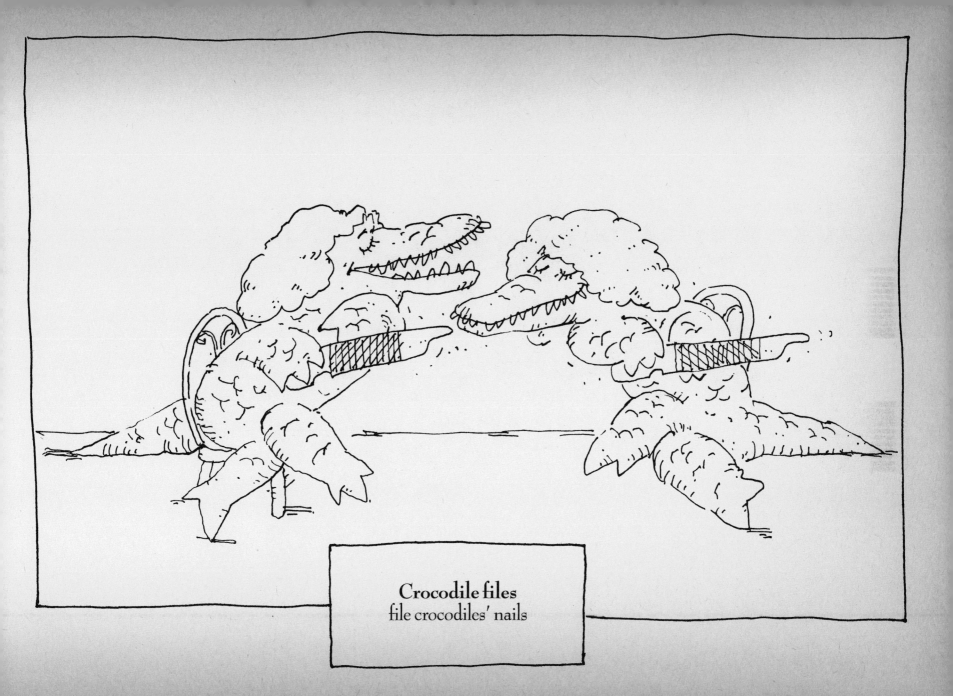

Crocodile files
file crocodiles' nails

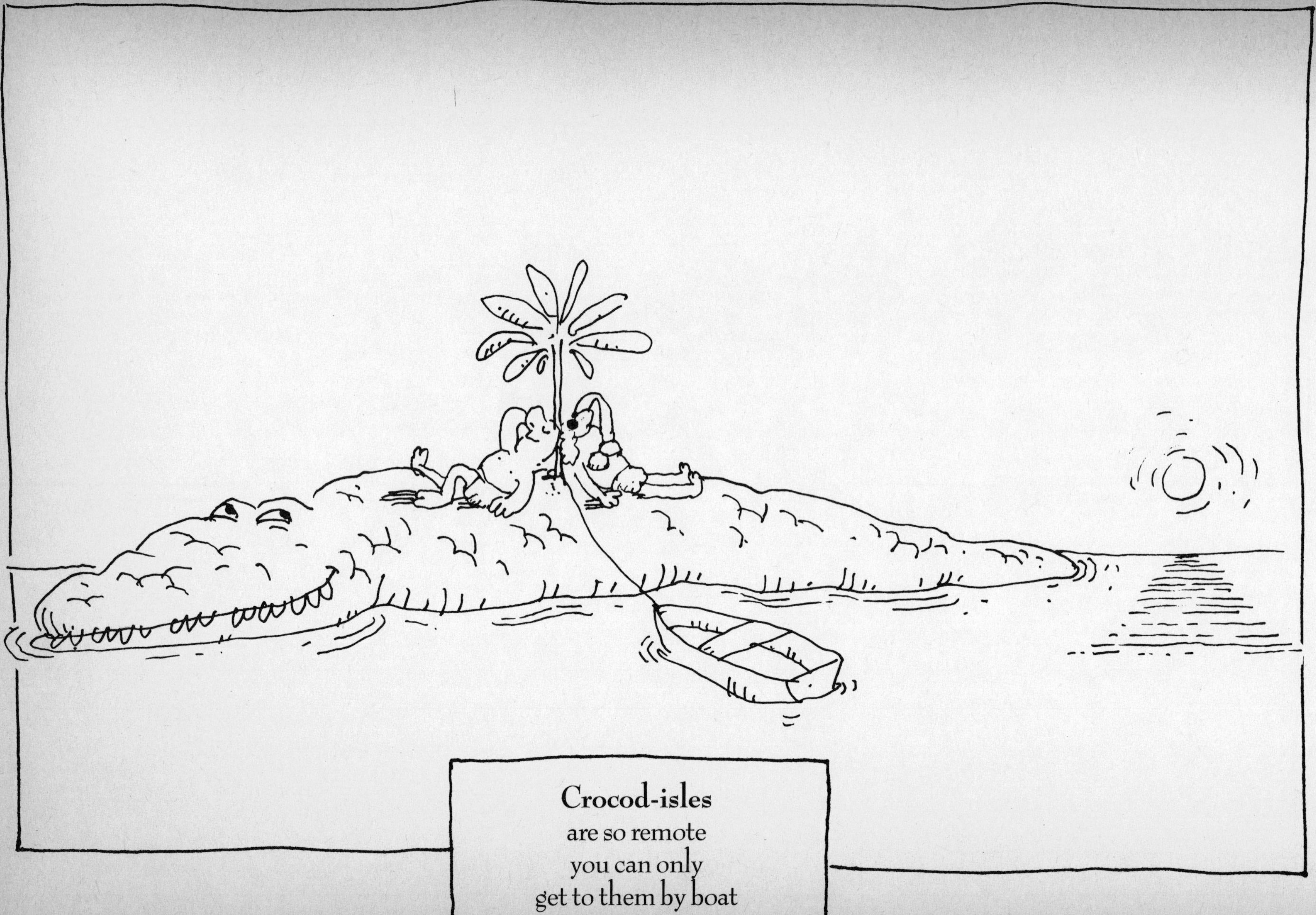

Crocod-isles
are so remote
you can only
get to them by boat

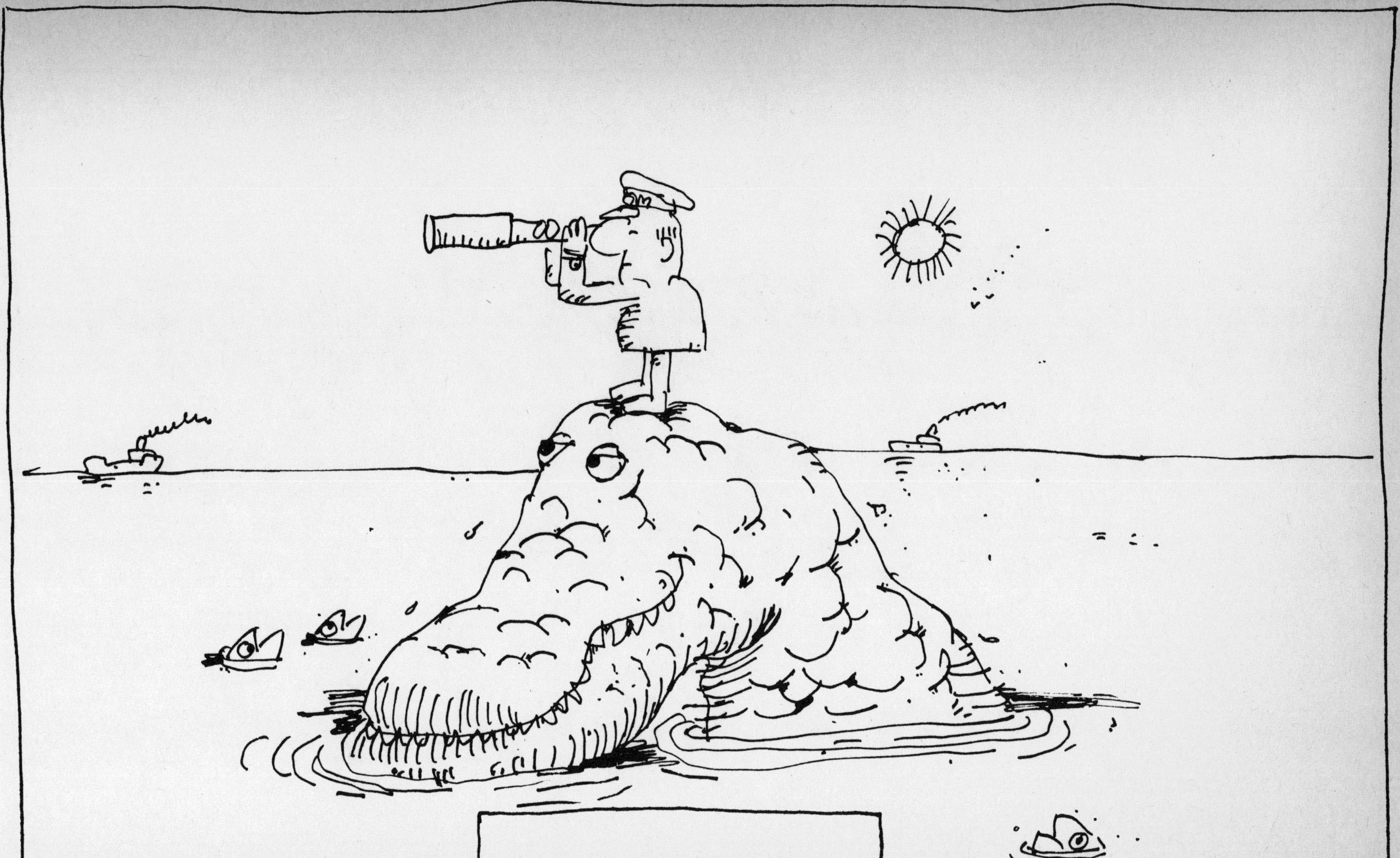

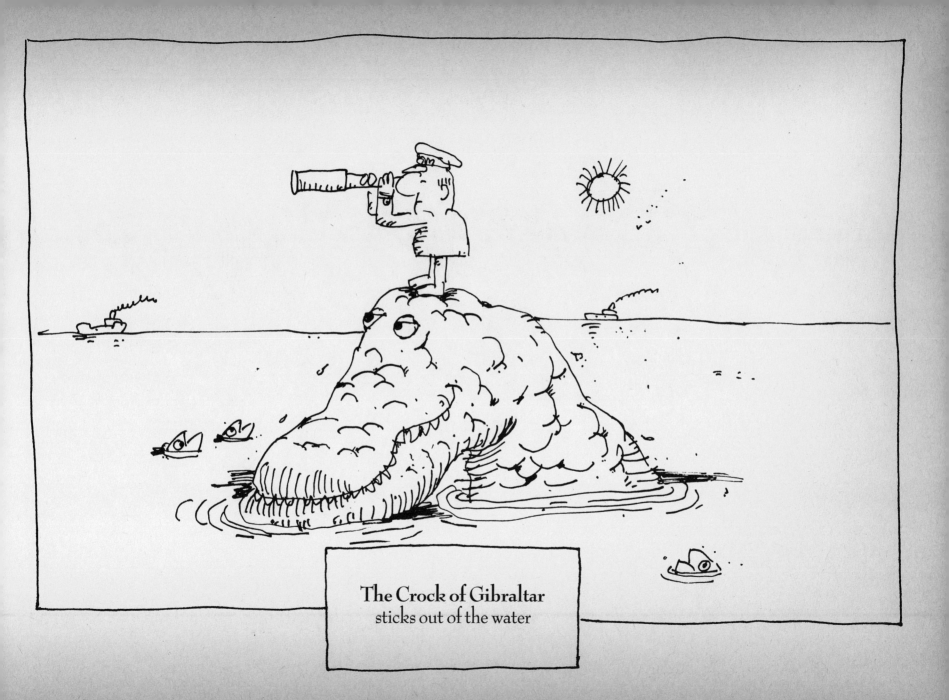

The Crock of Gibraltar
sticks out of the water

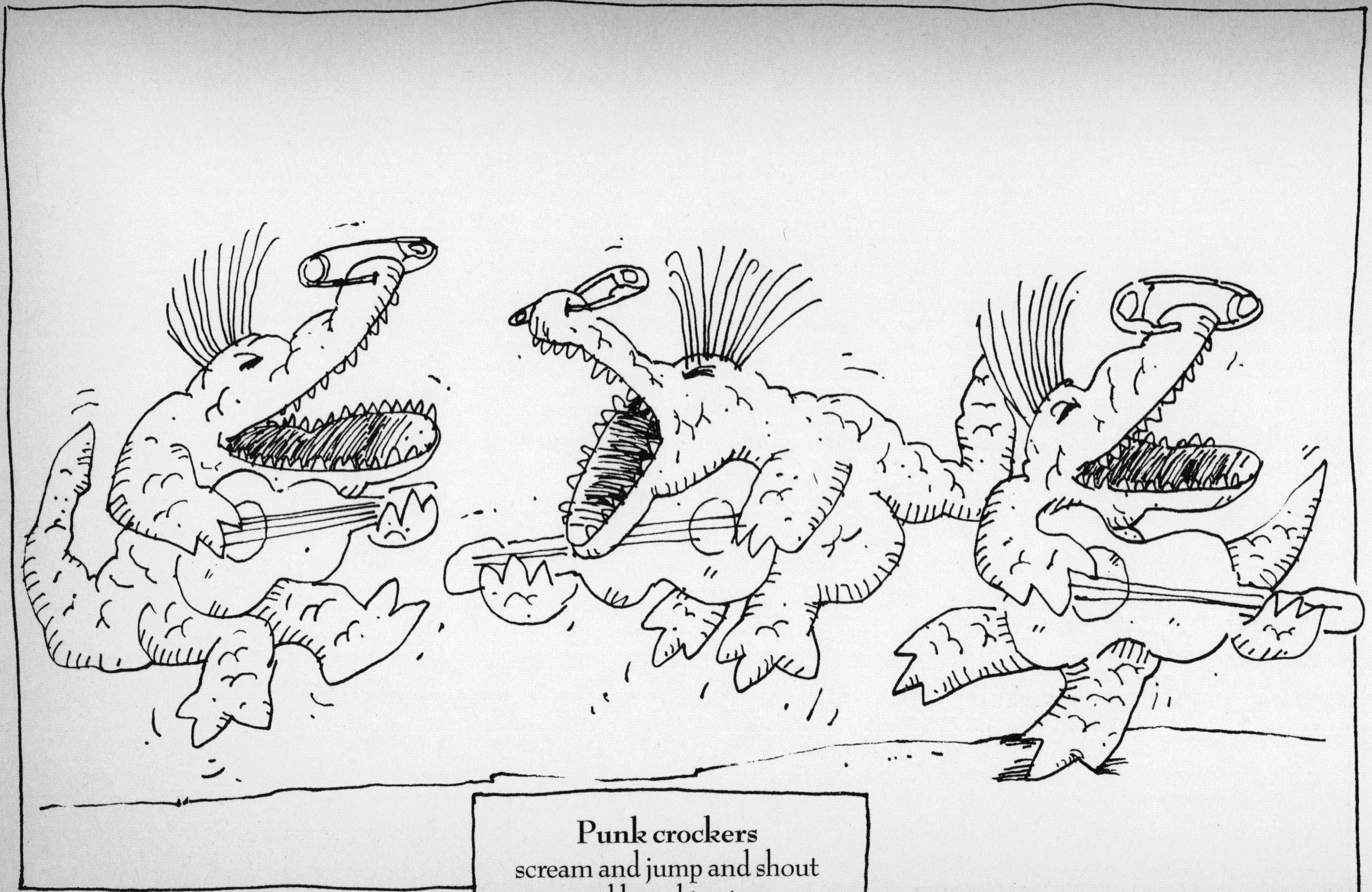

Punk crockers
scream and jump and shout
and have big pins
stuck through their snout

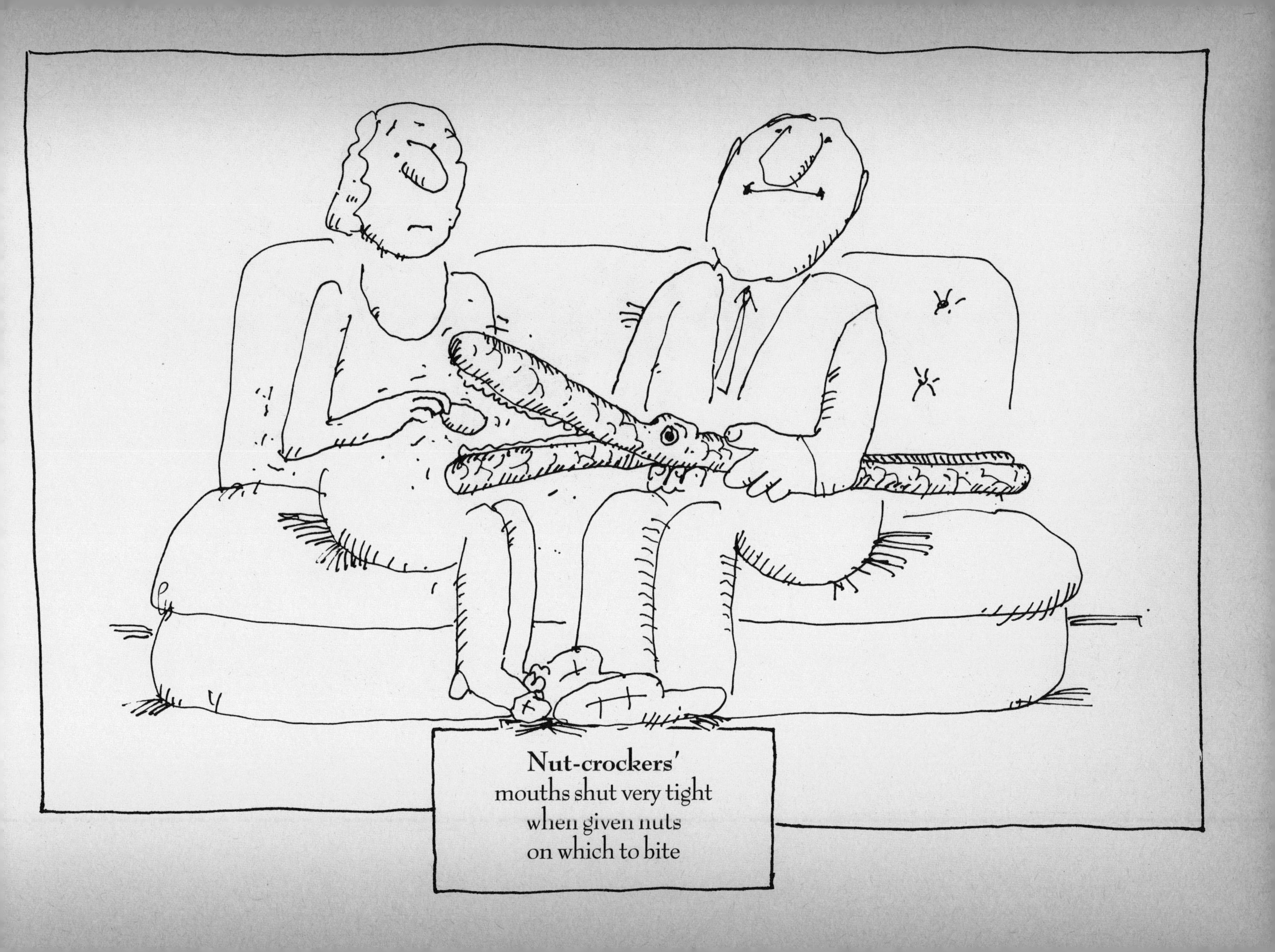

Nut-crockers'
mouths shut very tight
when given nuts
on which to bite

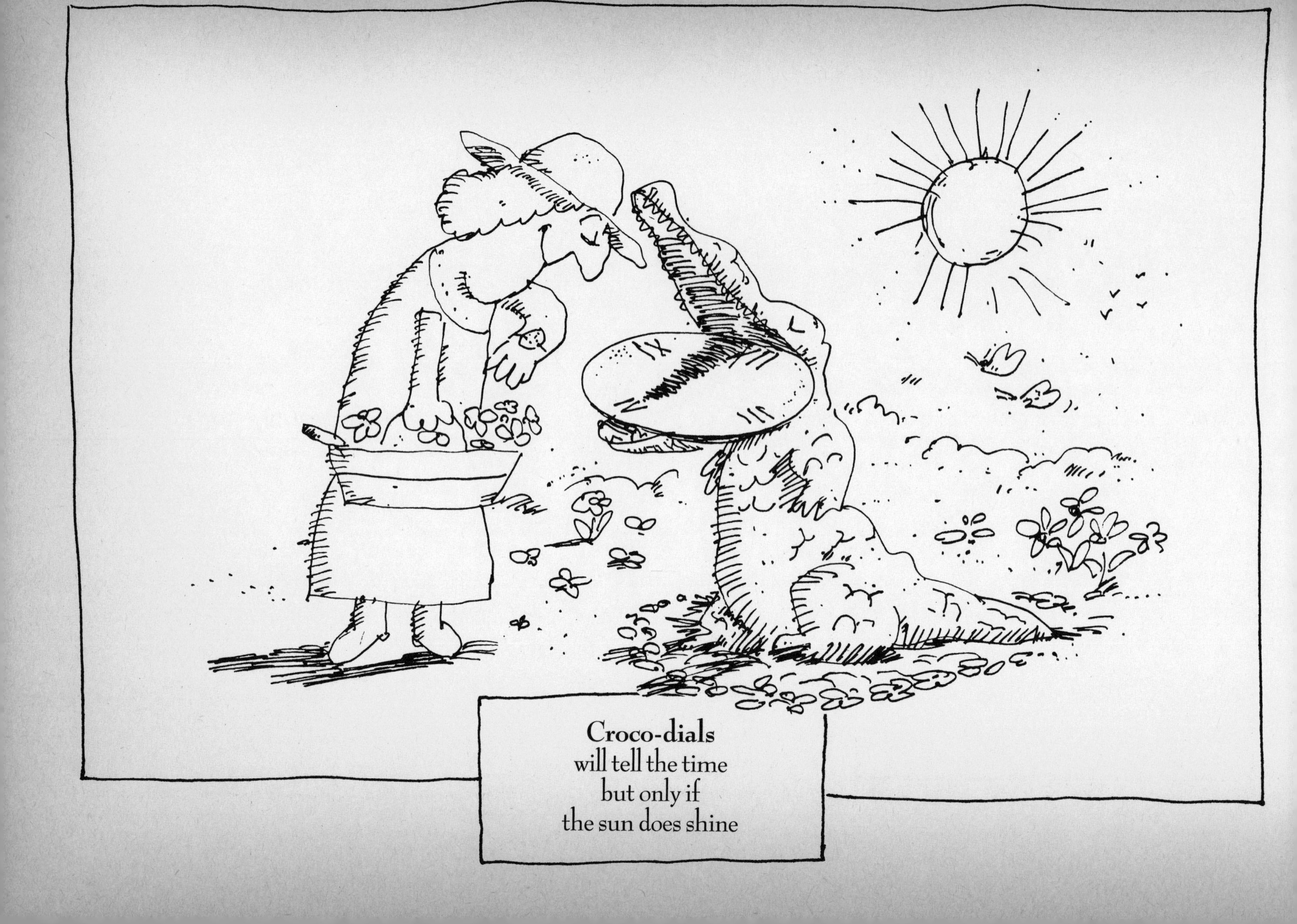

Croco-dials
will tell the time
but only if
the sun does shine

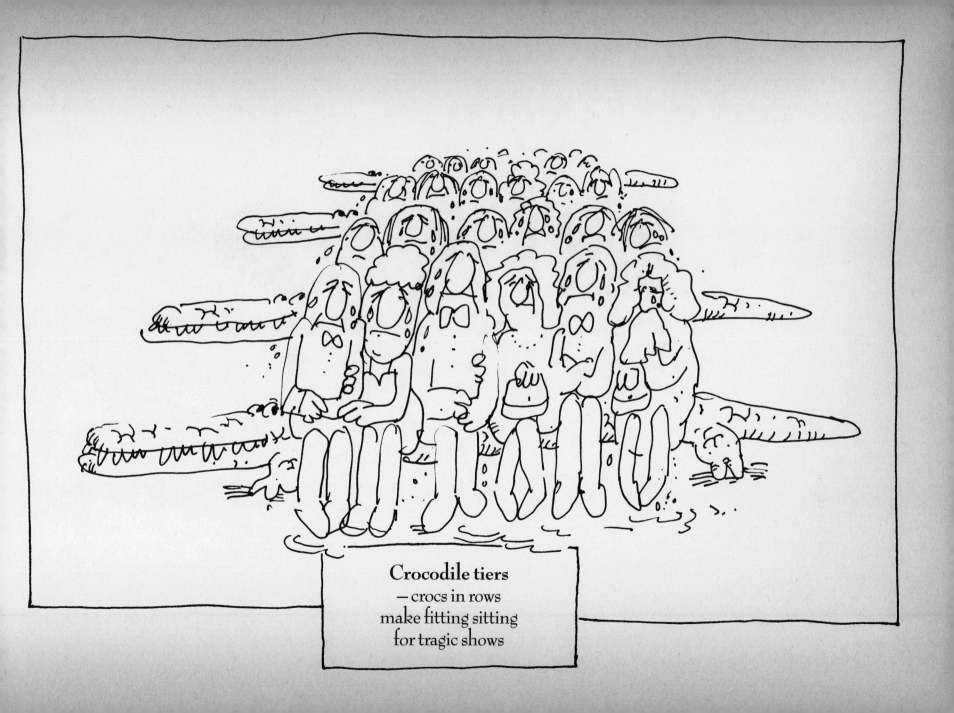

Crocodile tiers
— crocs in rows
make fitting sitting
for tragic shows

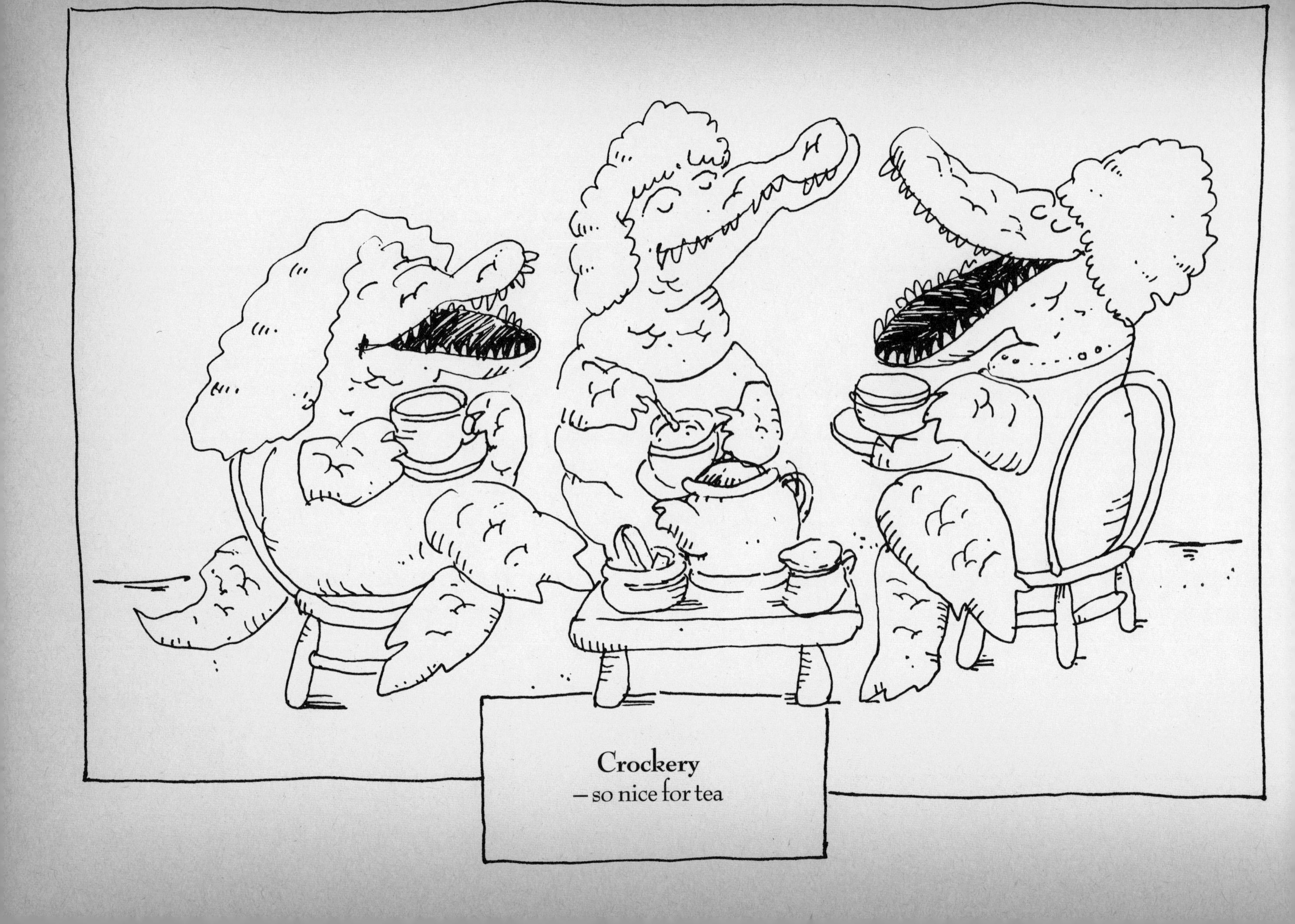

Crockery
– so nice for tea

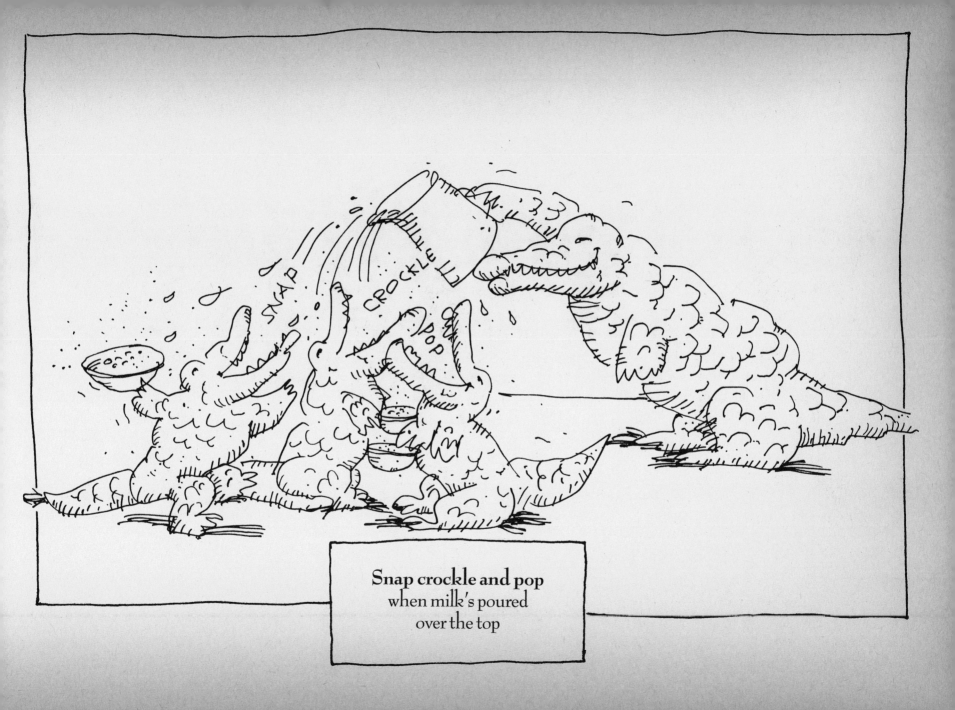

Snap crockle and pop
when milk's poured
over the top

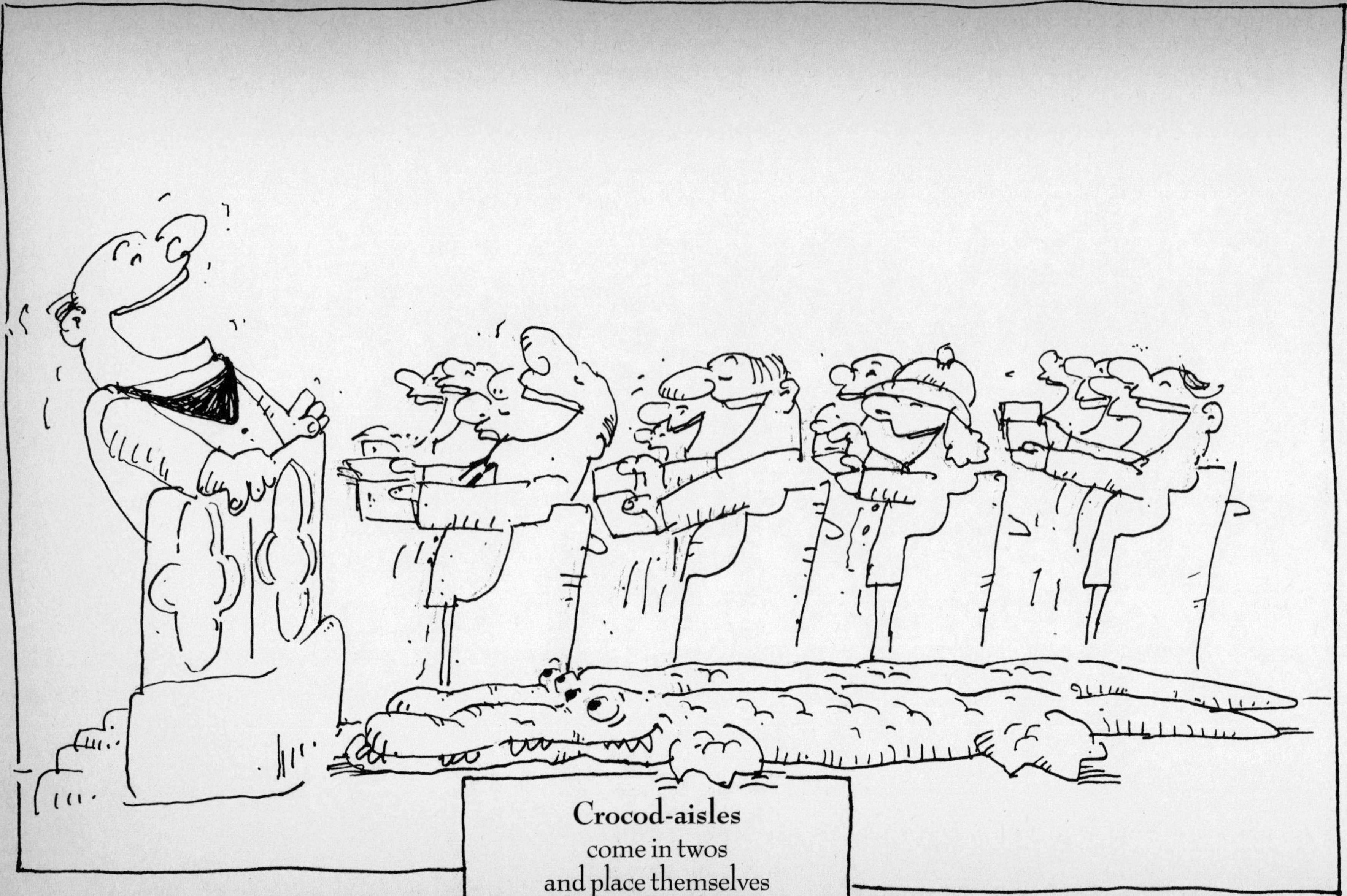

Crocod-aisles
come in twos
and place themselves
between the pews

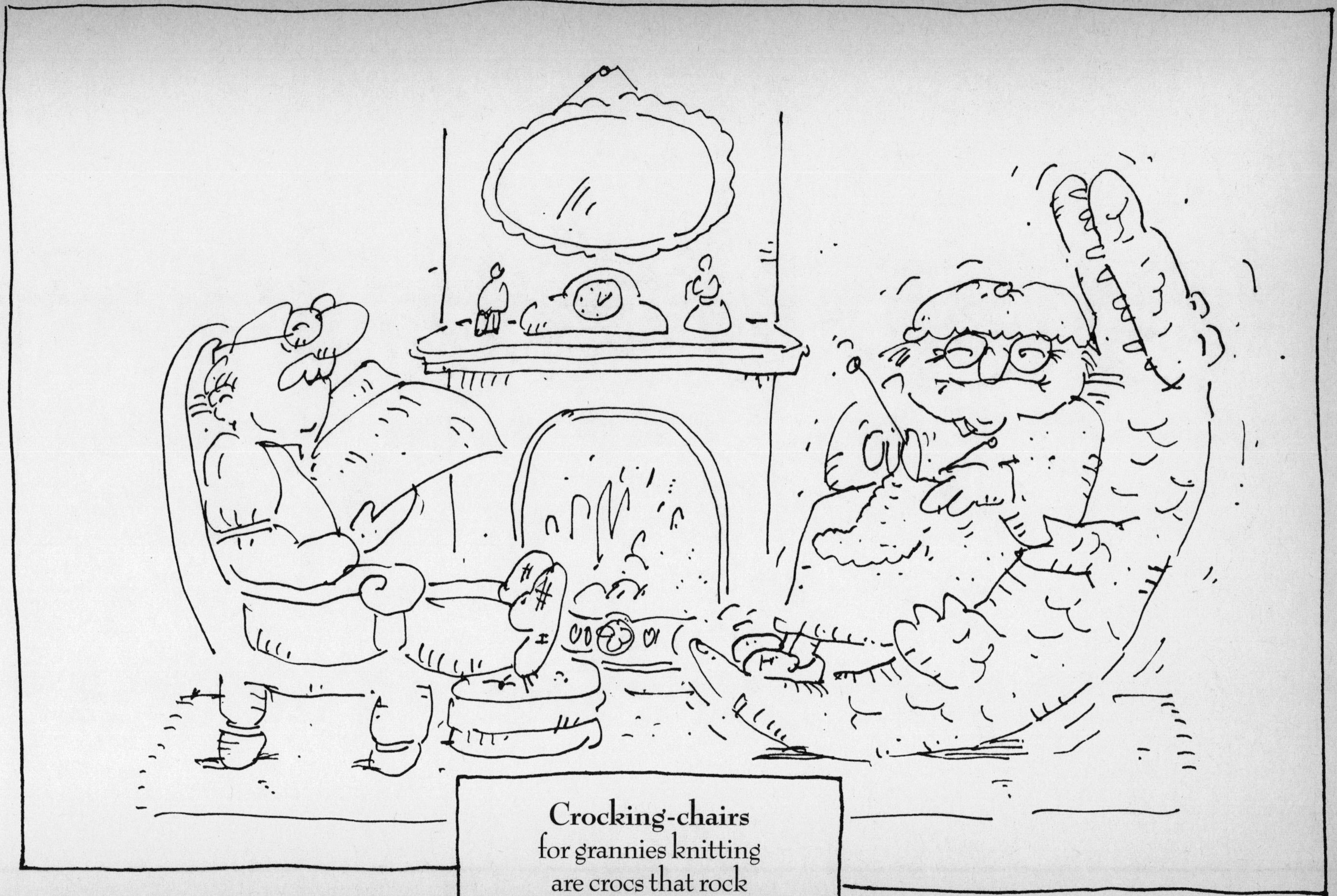

Crocking-chairs
for grannies knitting
are crocs that rock
for her to sit in

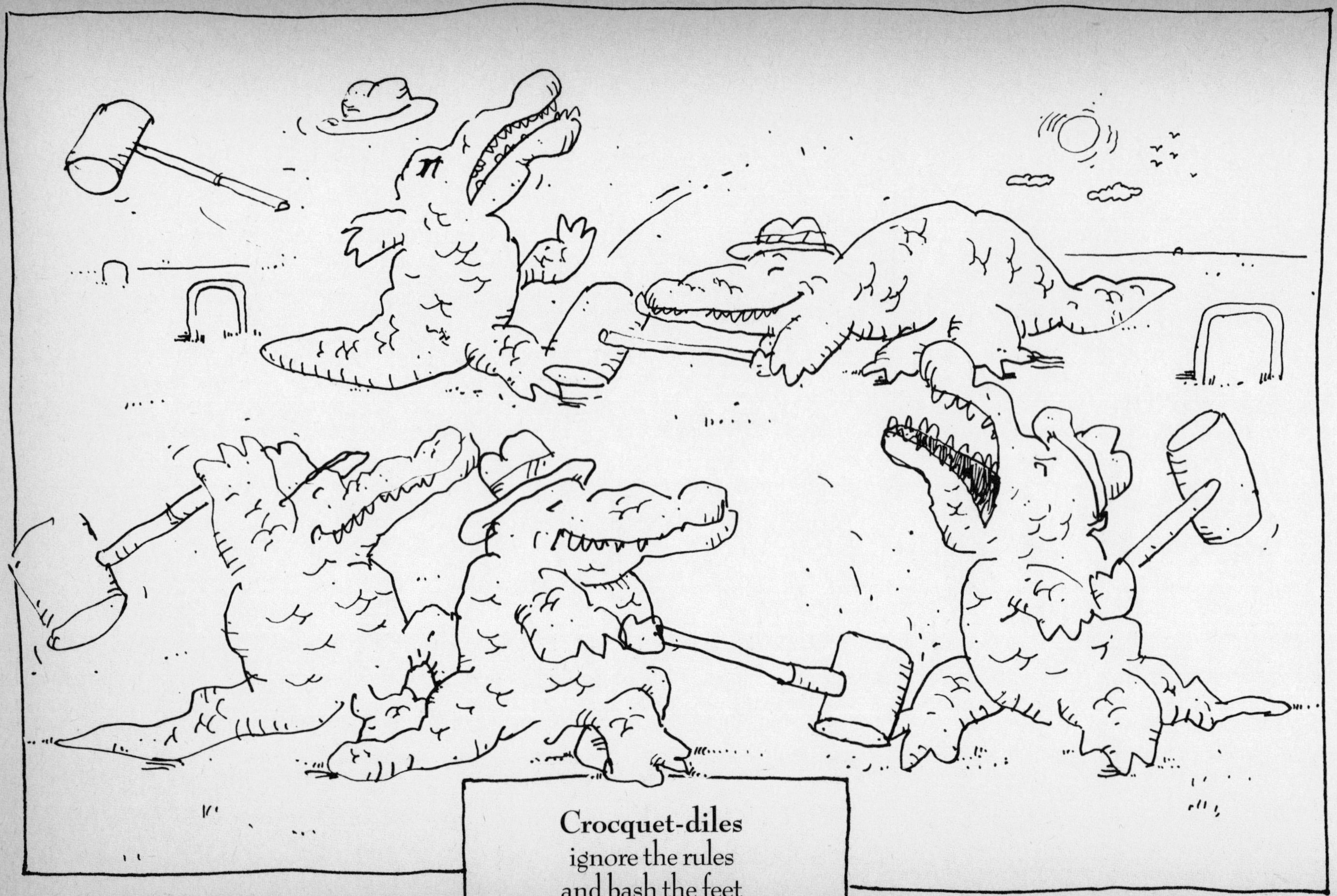

Crocquet-diles
ignore the rules
and bash the feet
as well as the balls

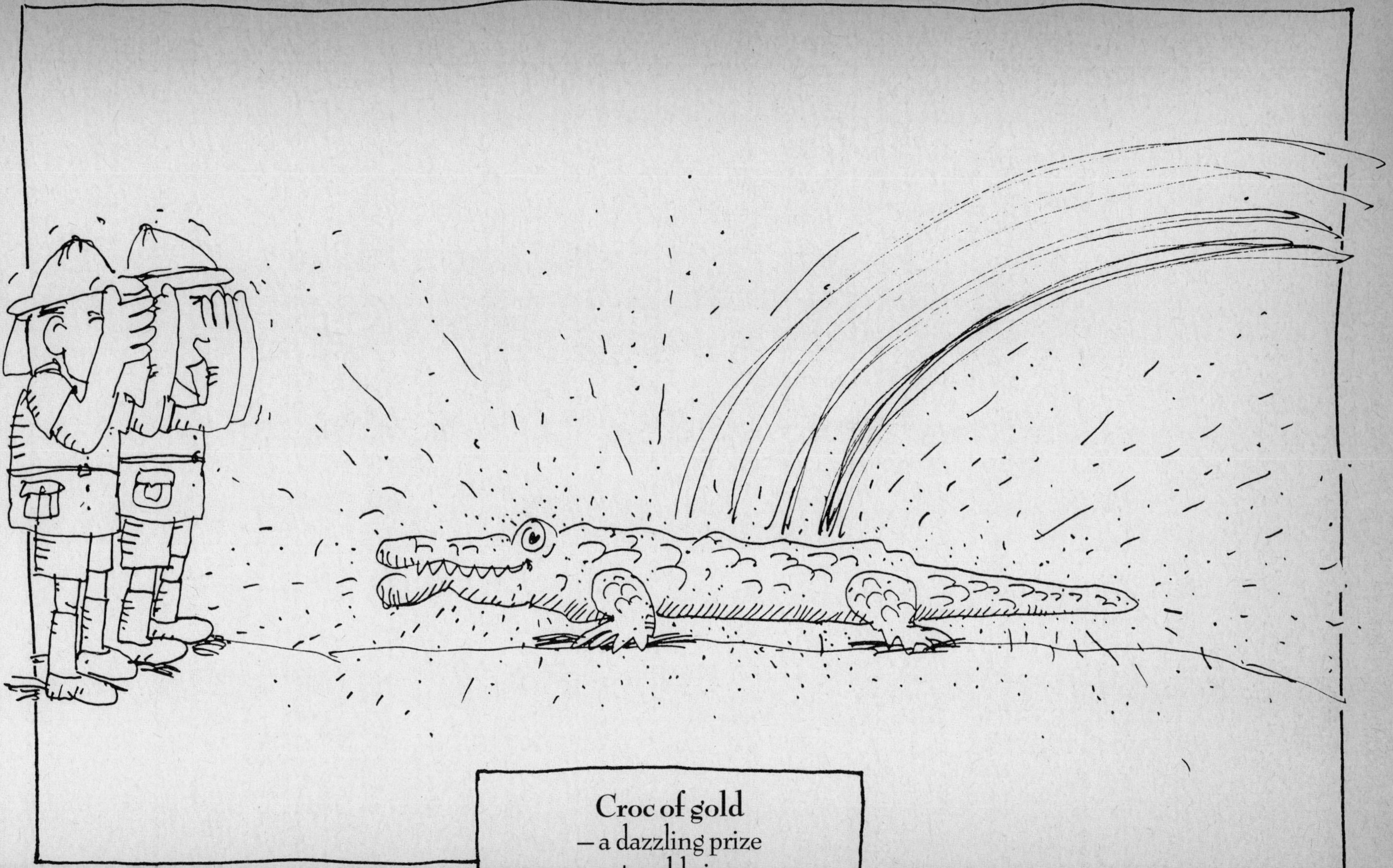

Croc of gold
– a dazzling prize
trouble is
it hurts your eyes

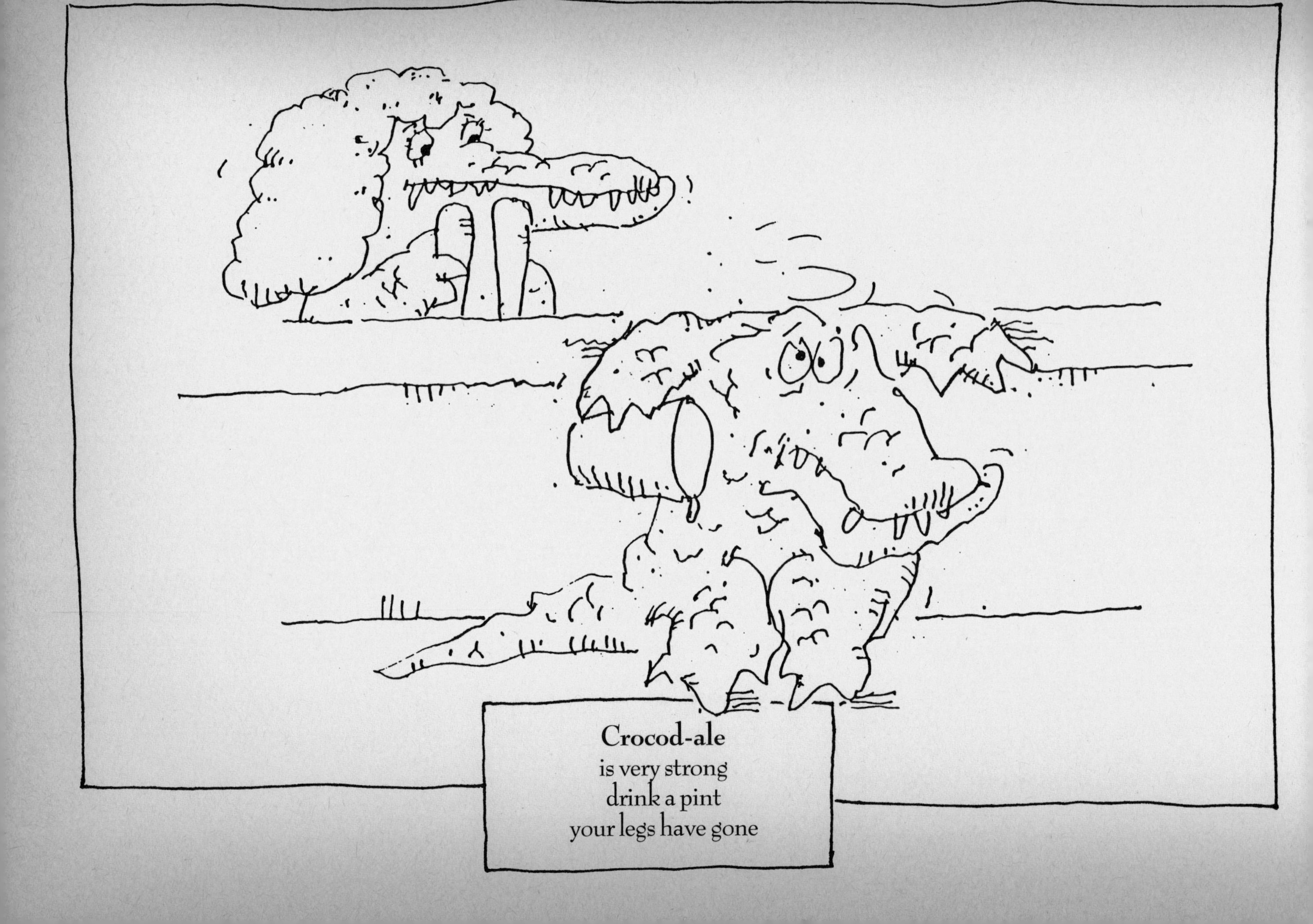

Crocod-ale

is very strong
drink a pint
your legs have gone

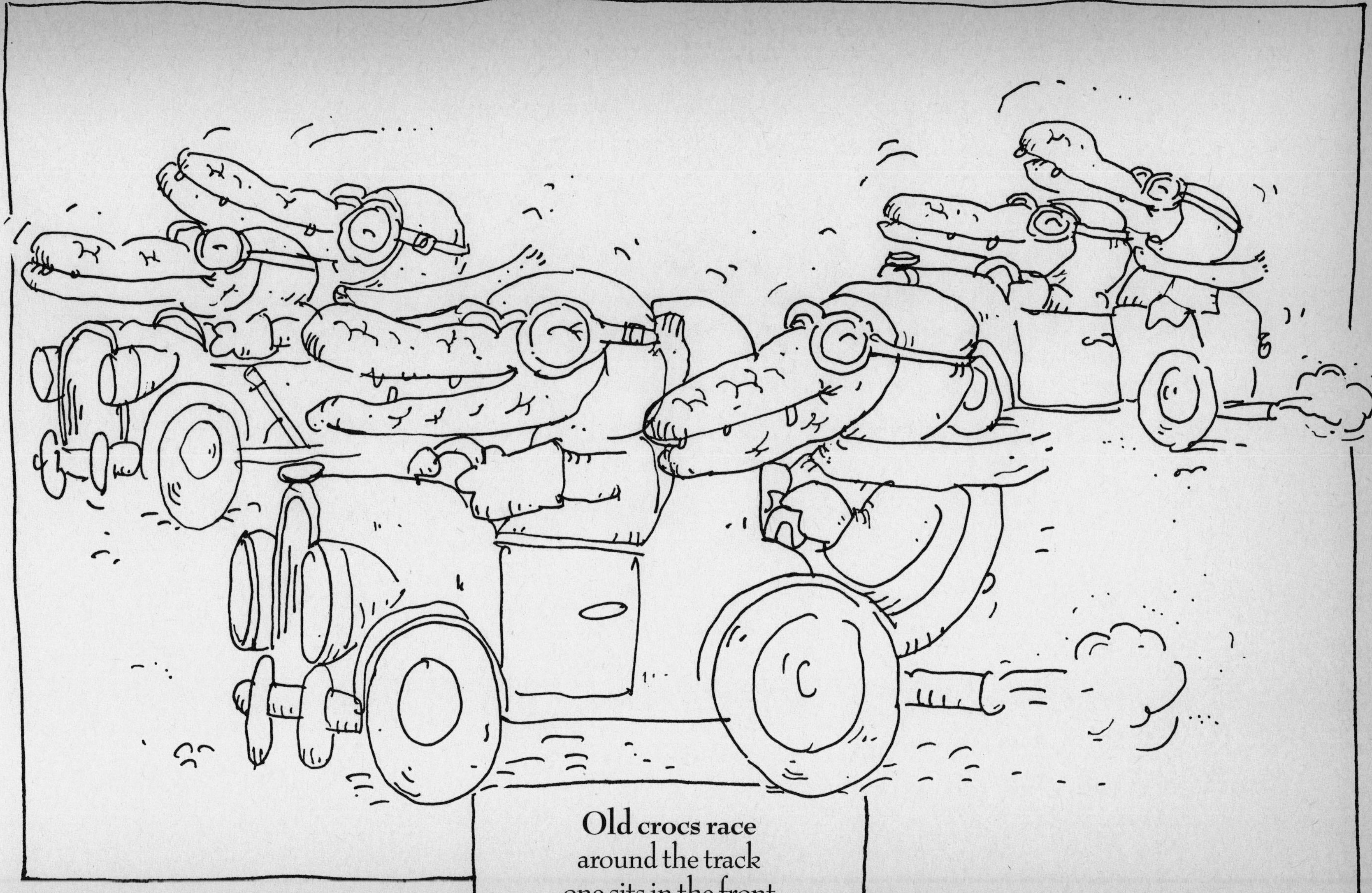

Old crocs race
around the track
one sits in the front
one sits in the back

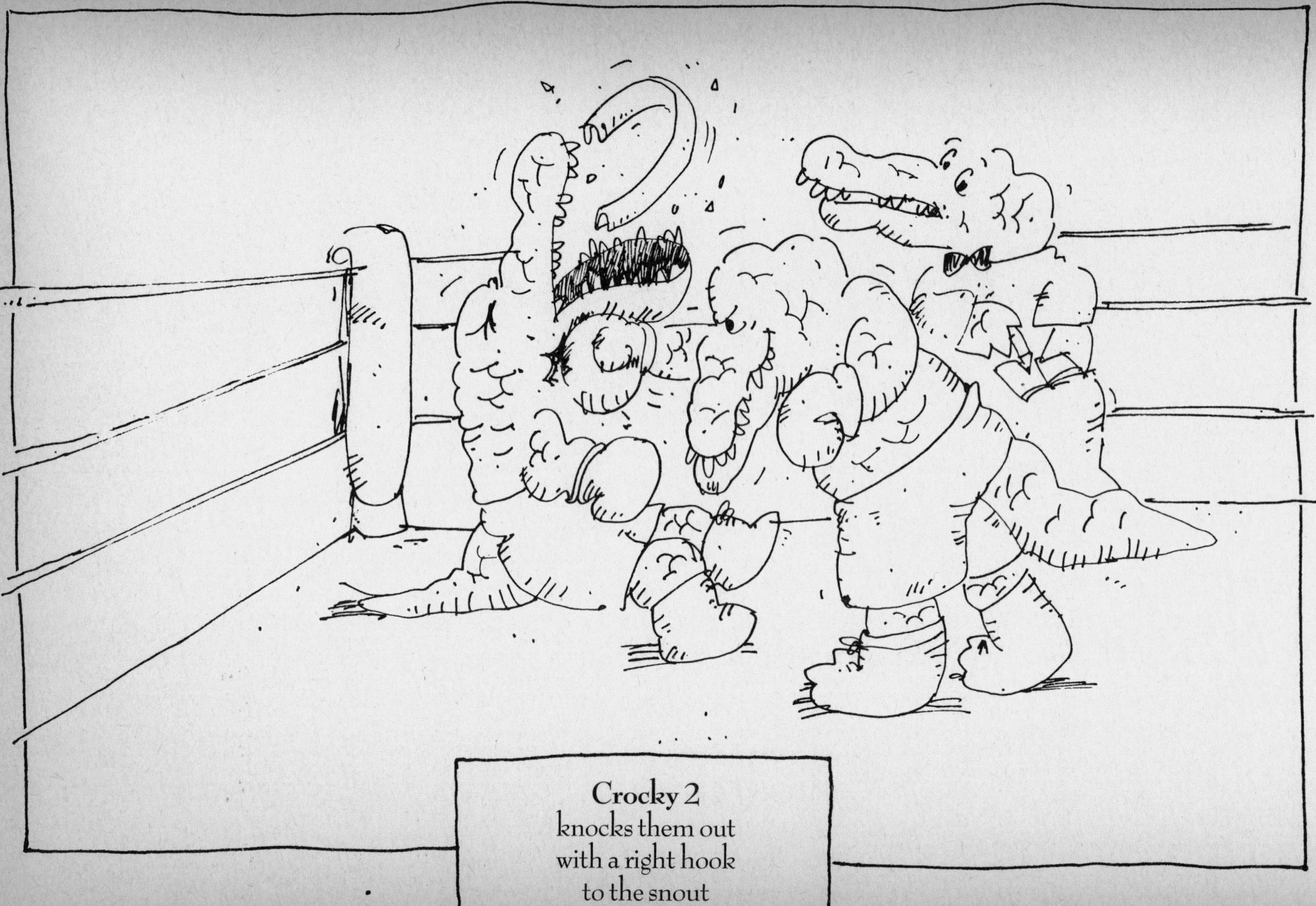

Crocky 2
knocks them out
with a right hook
to the snout

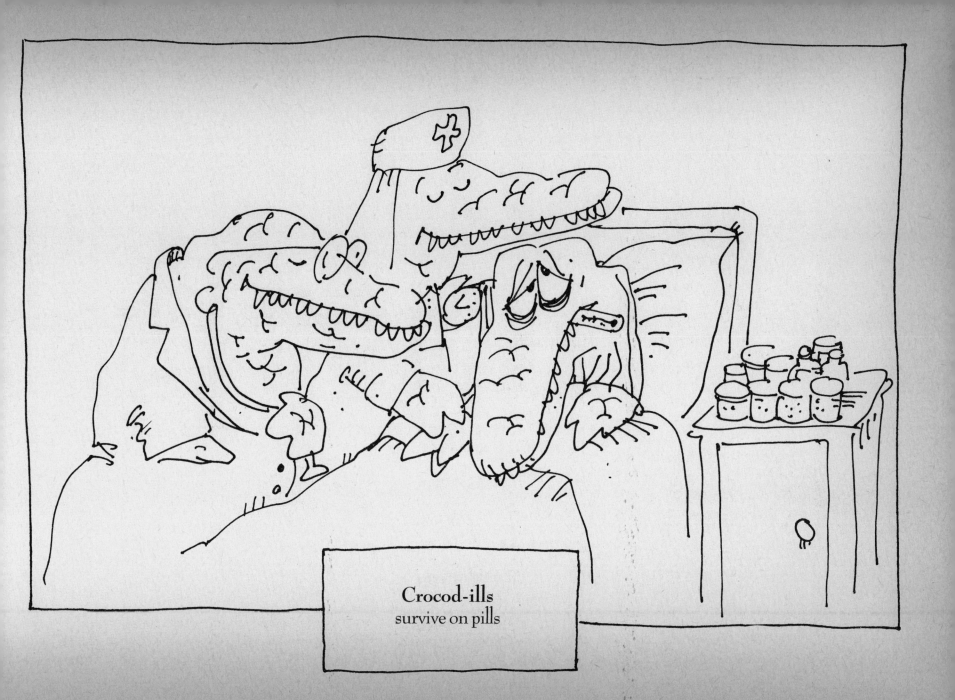

Crocod-ills
survive on pills

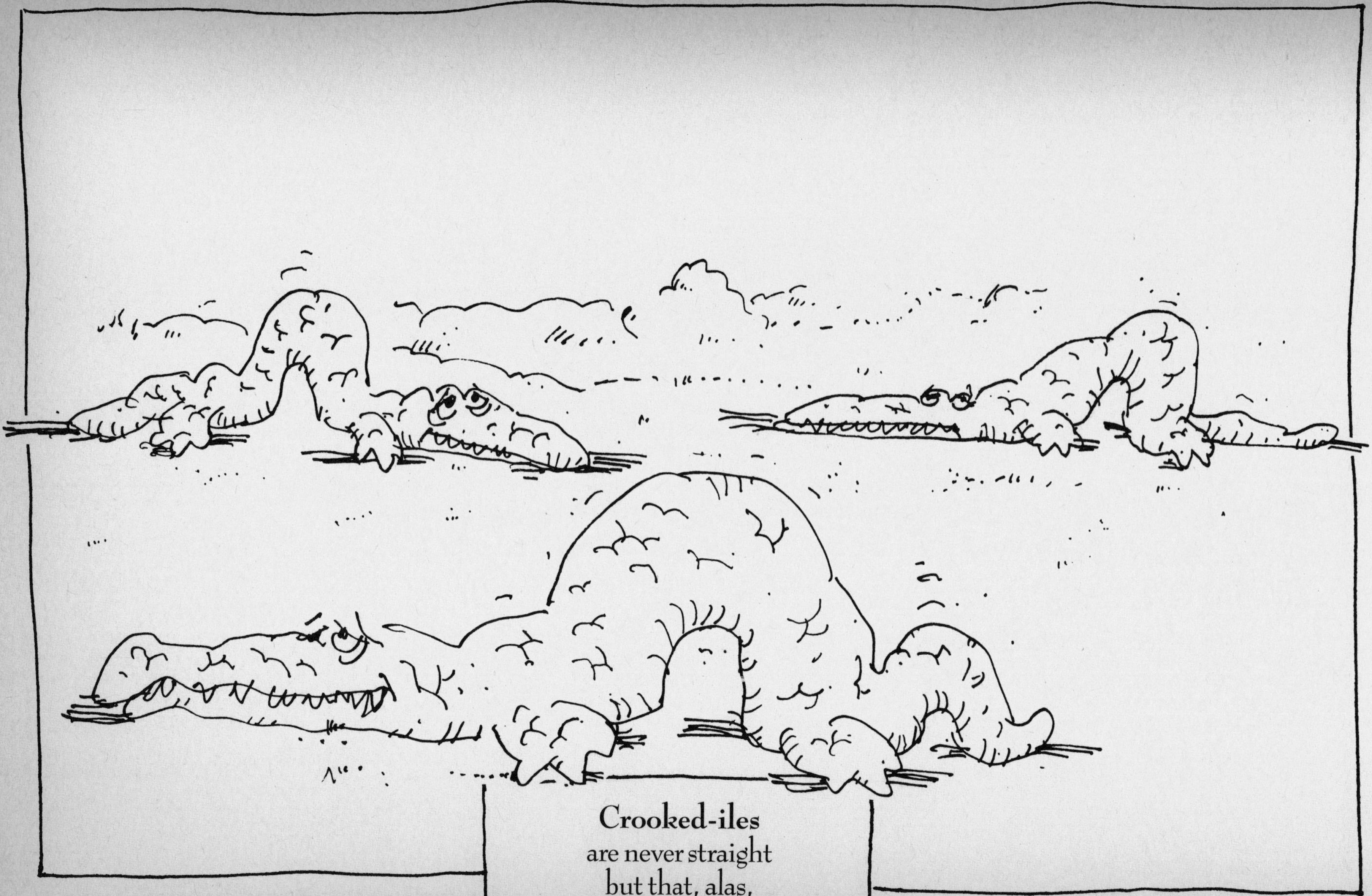

Crooked-iles
are never straight
but that, alas,
is their sad fate

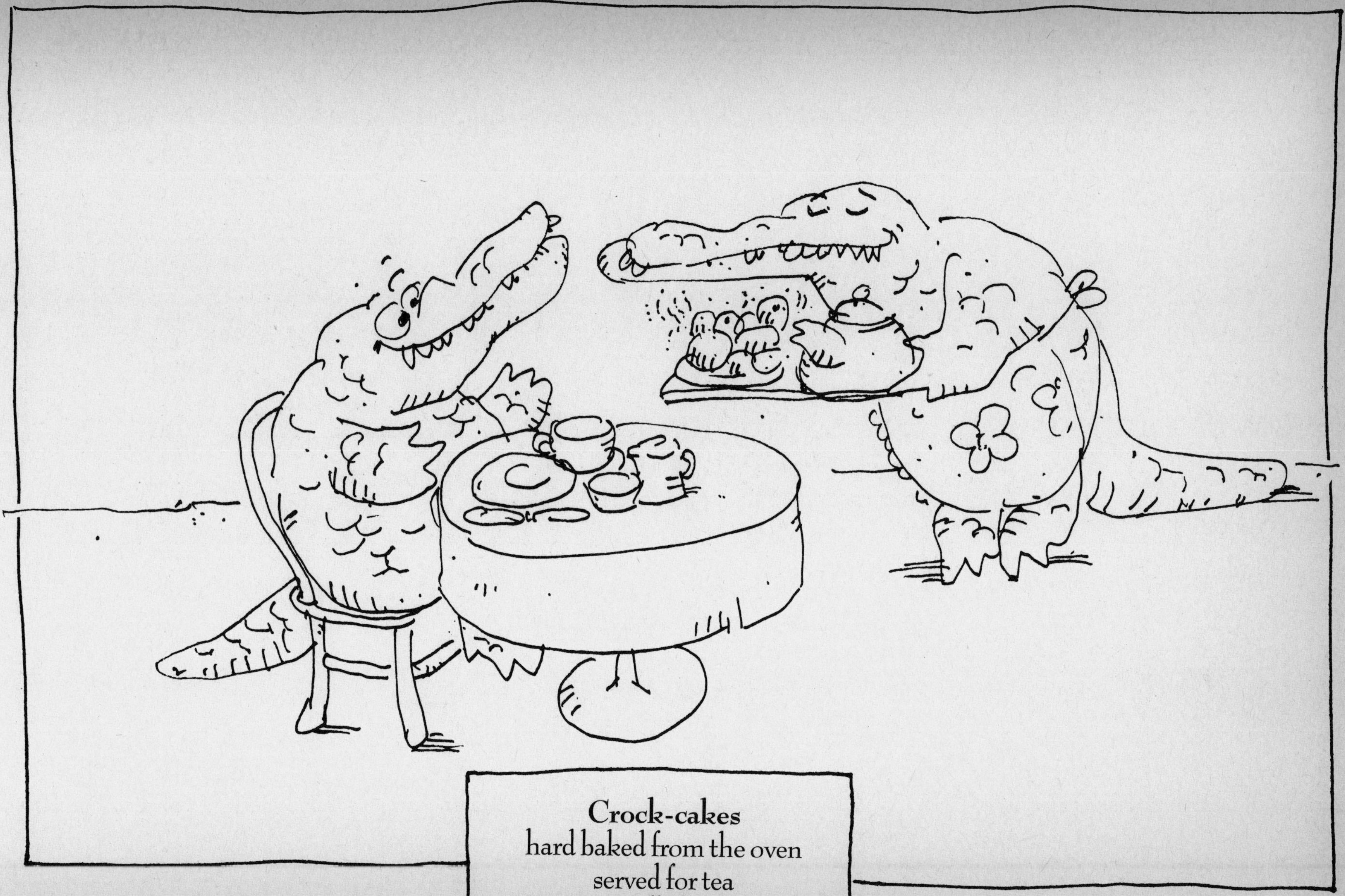

Crock-cakes
hard baked from the oven
served for tea
crocs really love 'em

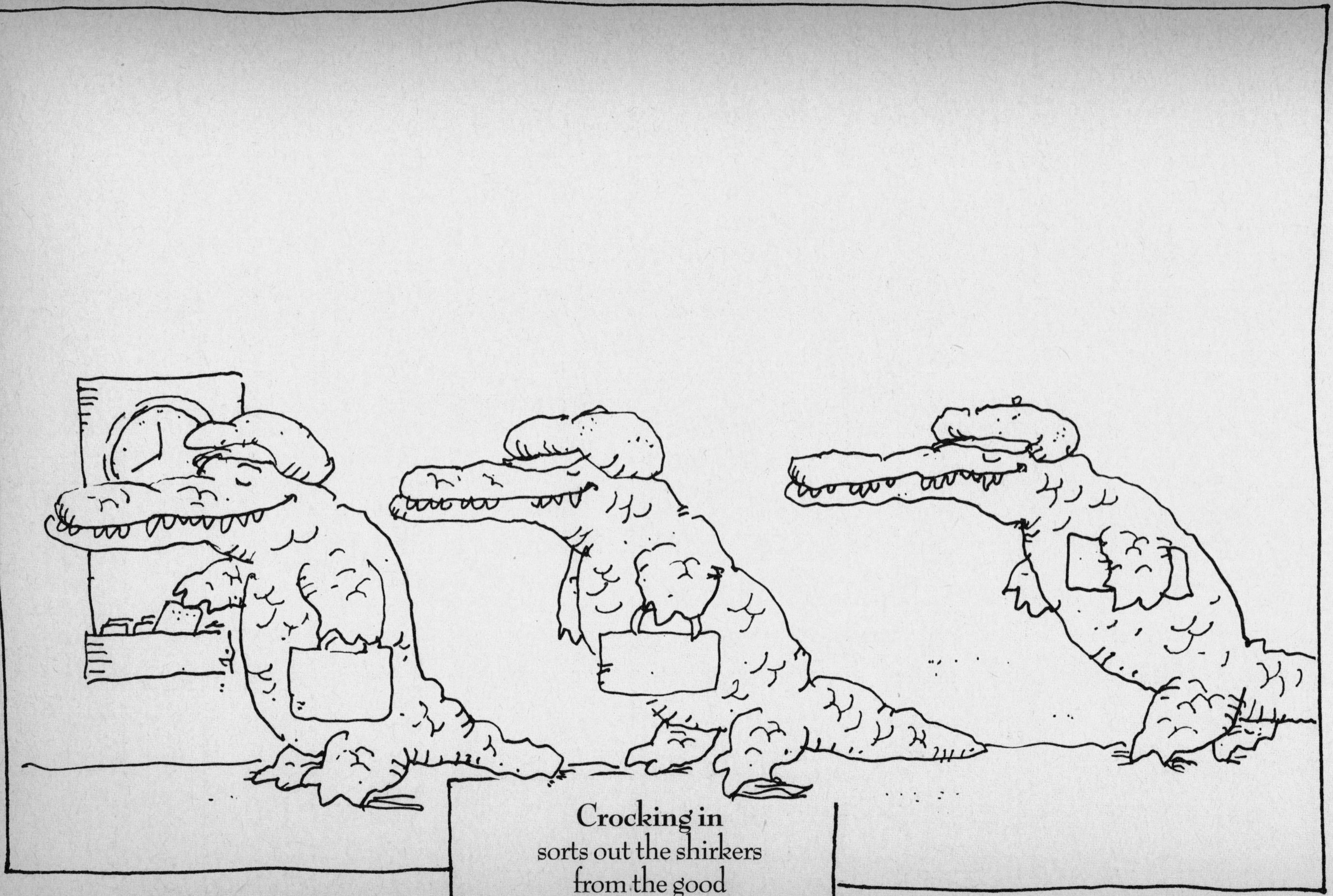

Crocking in
sorts out the shirkers
from the good
and honest workers

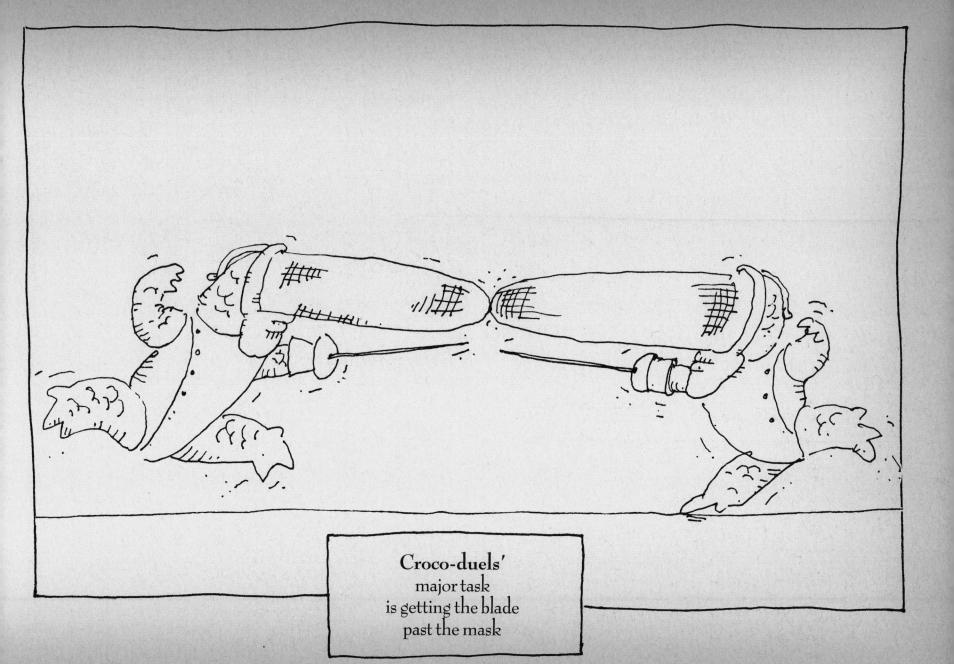

Croco-duels'
major task
is getting the blade
past the mask

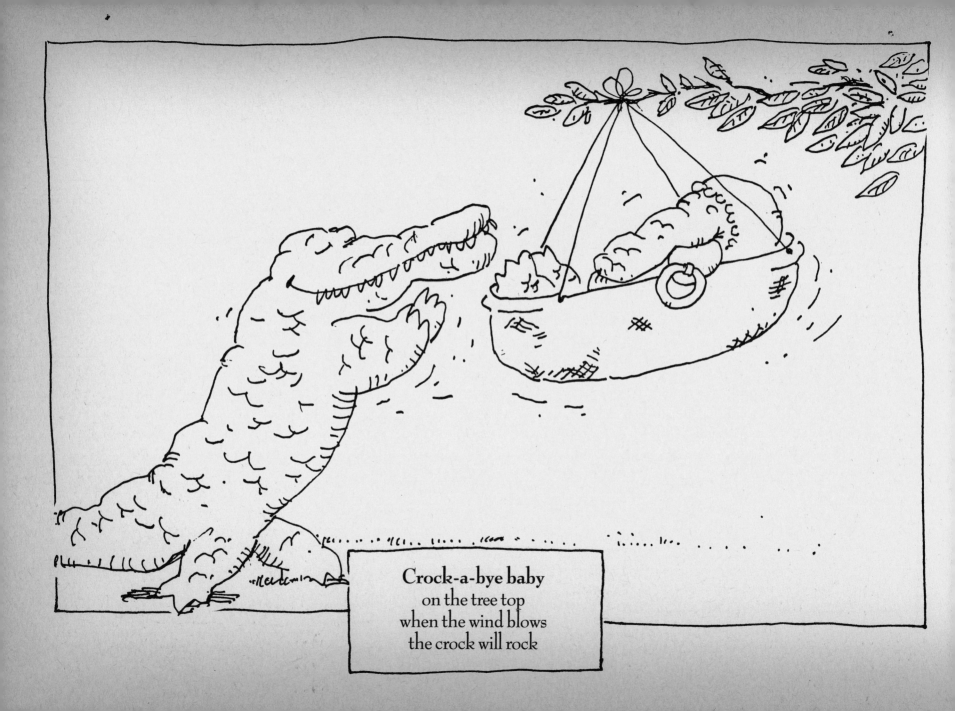

Crock-a-bye baby
on the tree top
when the wind blows
the crock will rock

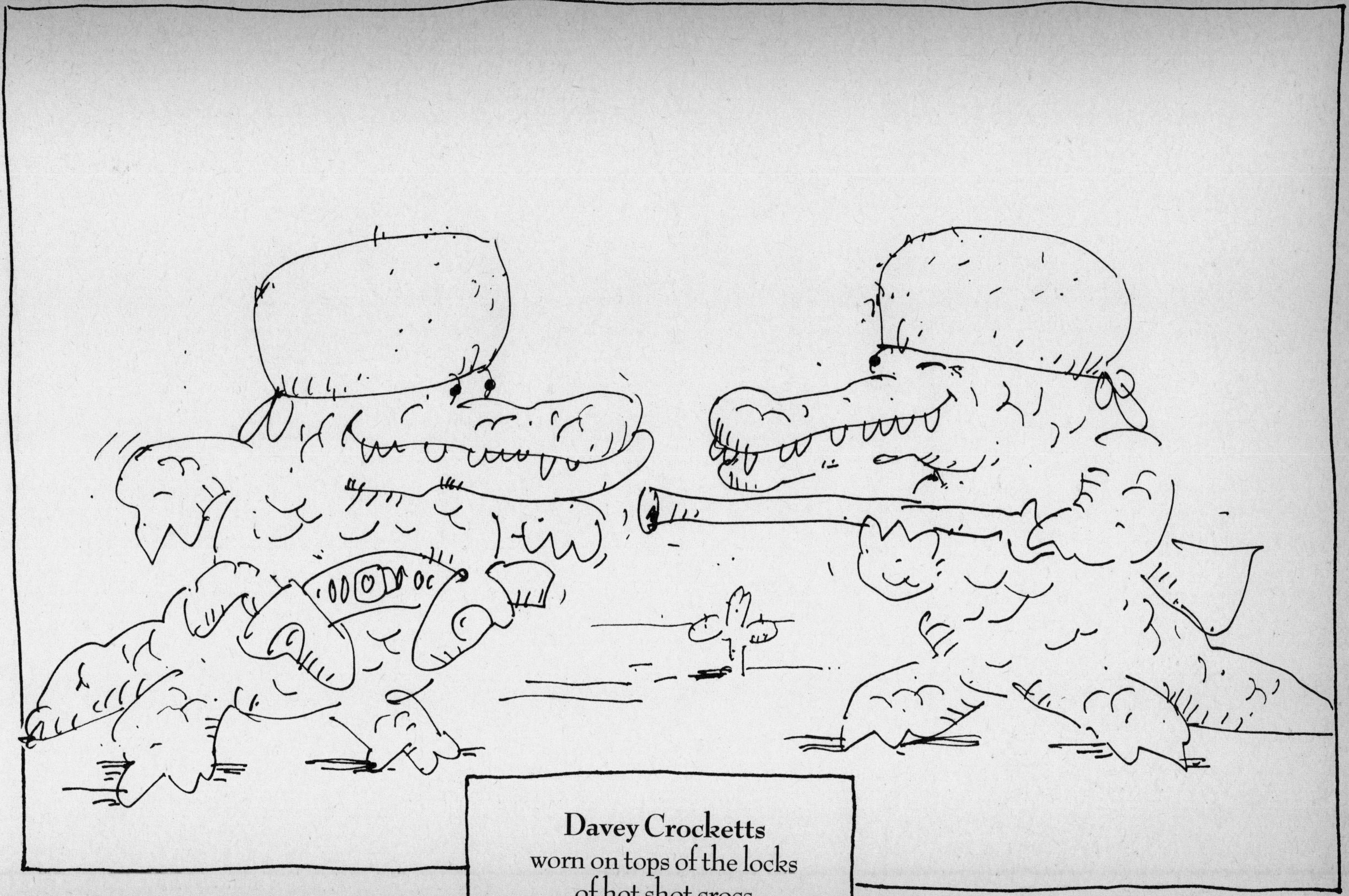

Davey Crocketts
worn on tops of the locks
of hot shot crocs

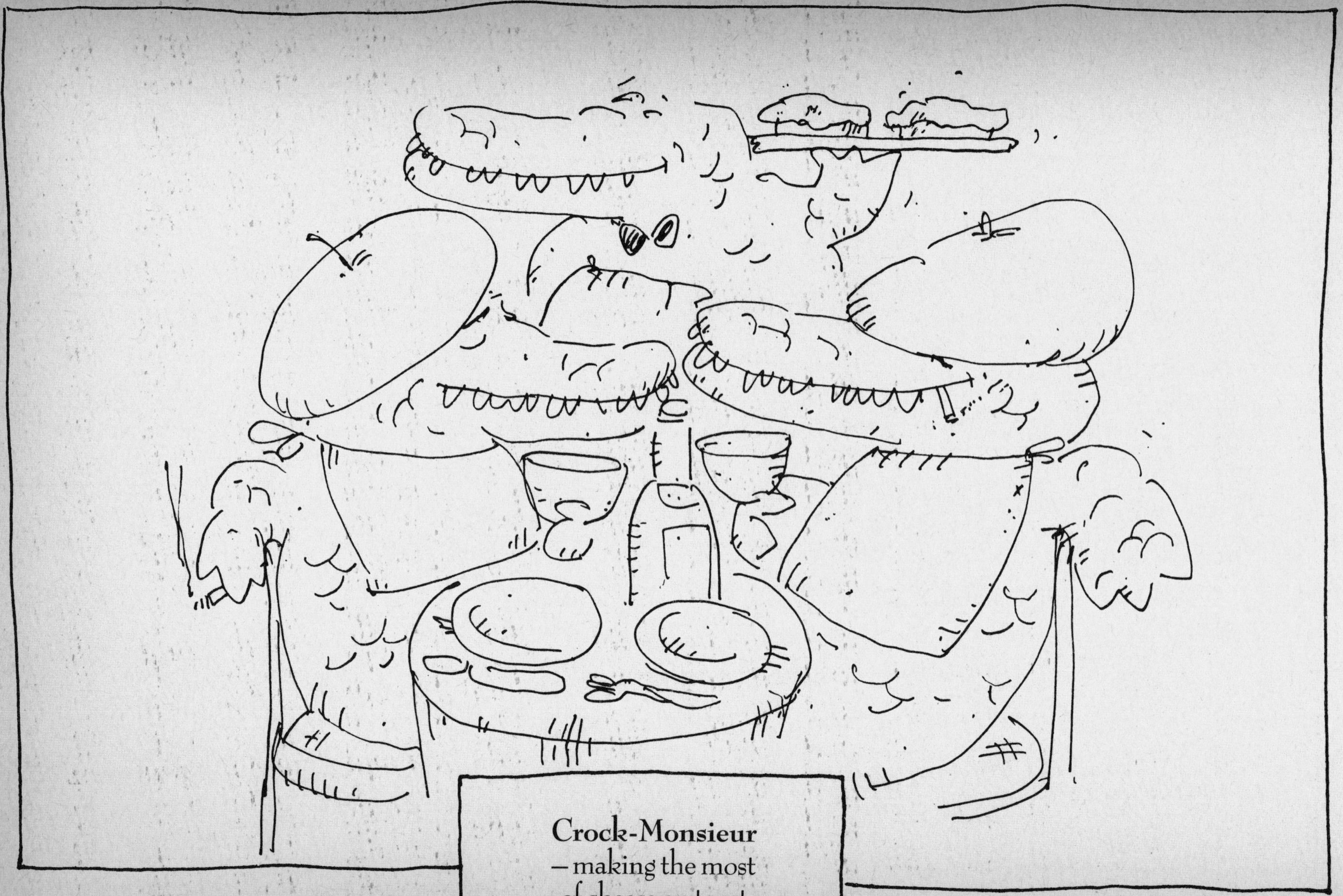

Crock-Monsieur
– making the most
of cheese on toast

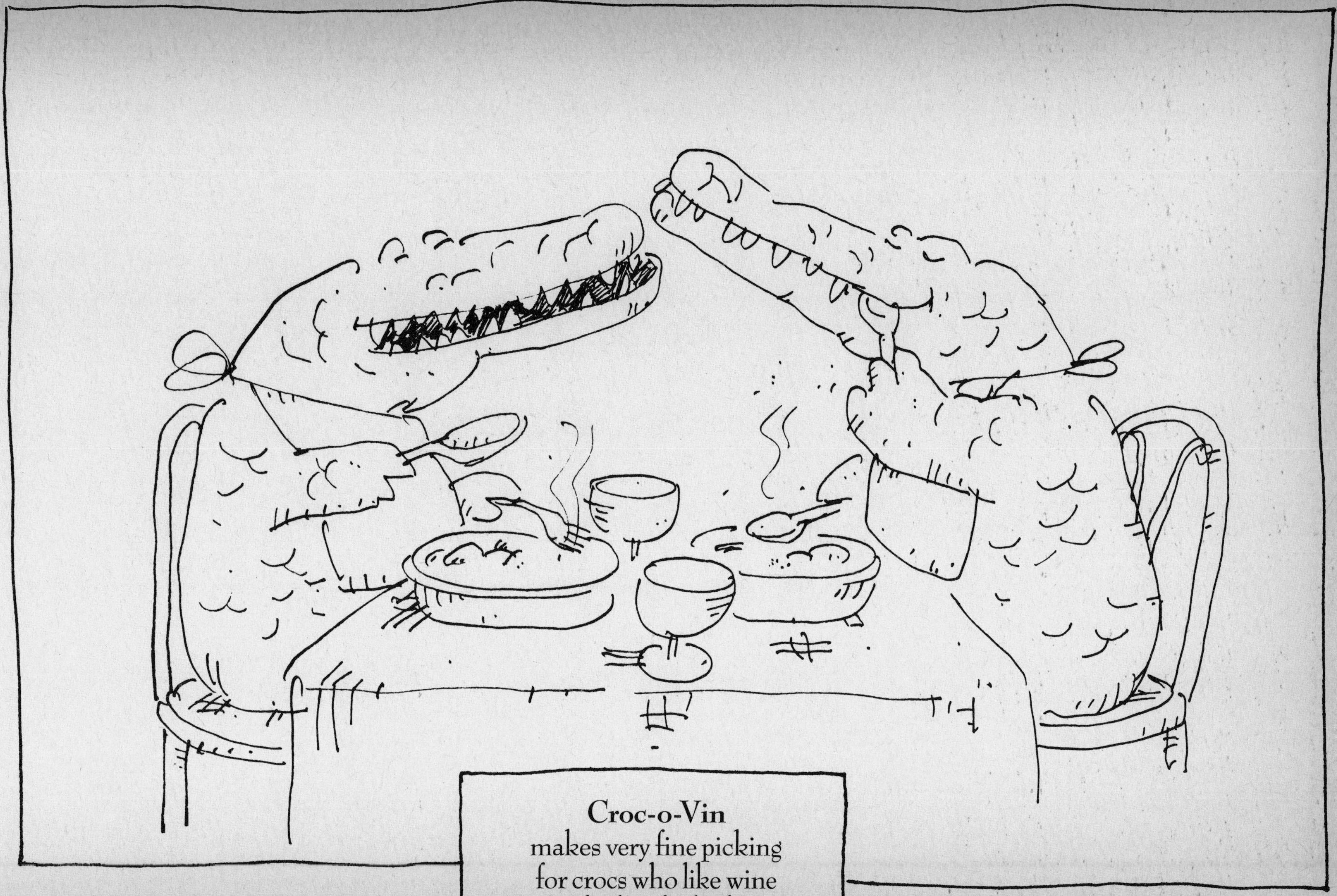

Croc-o-Vin
makes very fine picking
for crocs who like wine
cooked with chicken

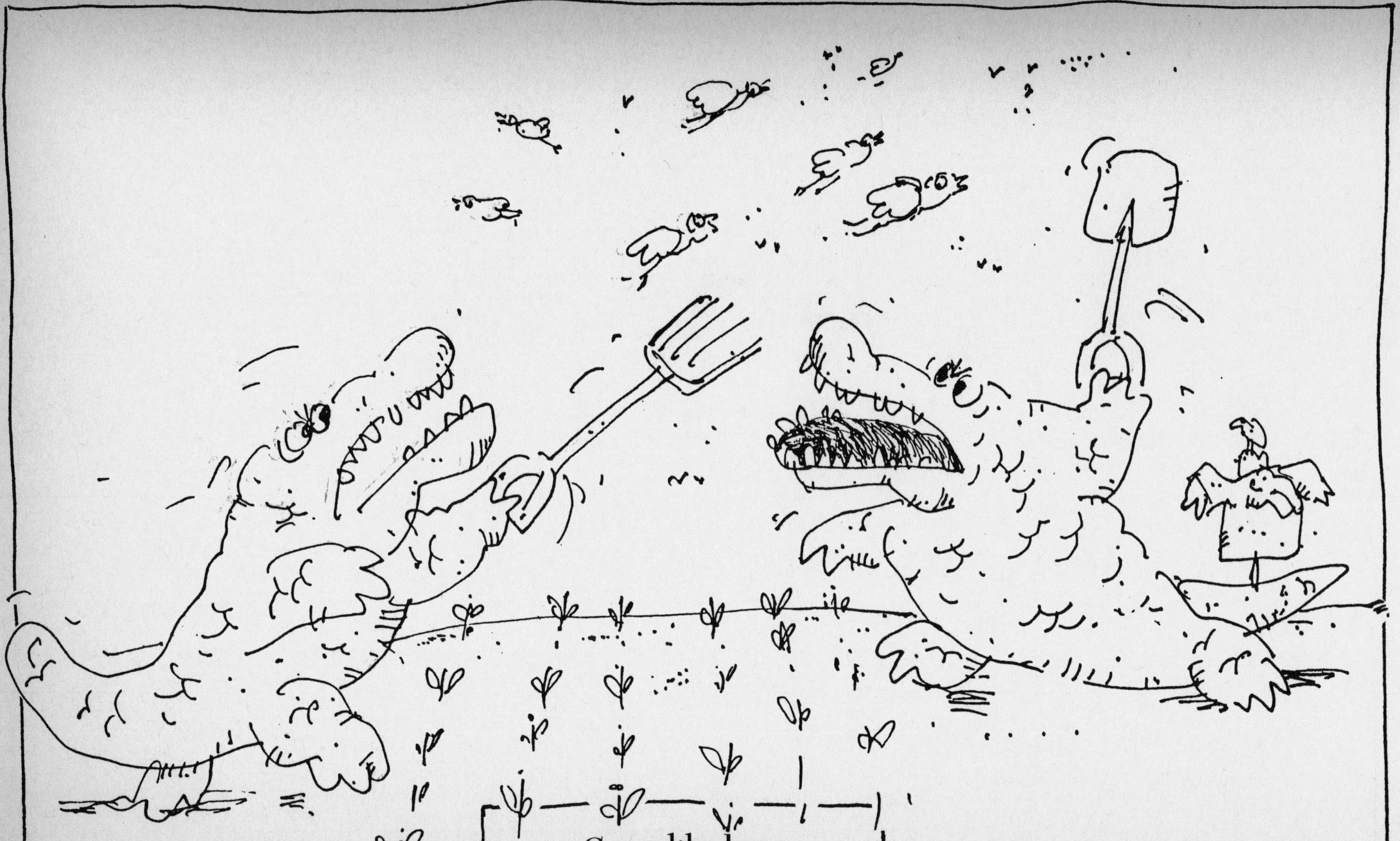

Crocodile shoes
away the birds
not with shoes that are worn
but with shoos that are heard

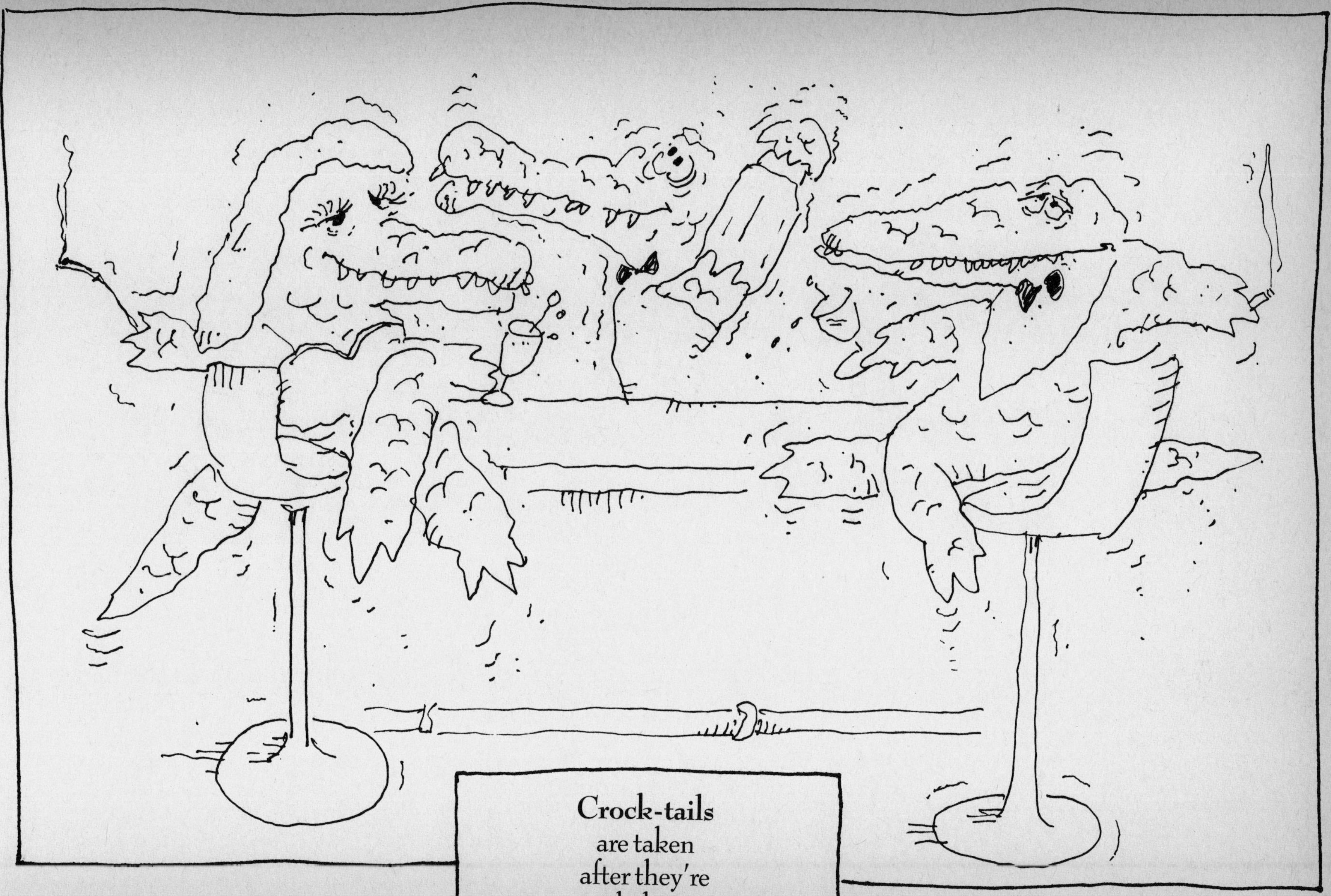

Crock-tails
are taken
after they're
shaken

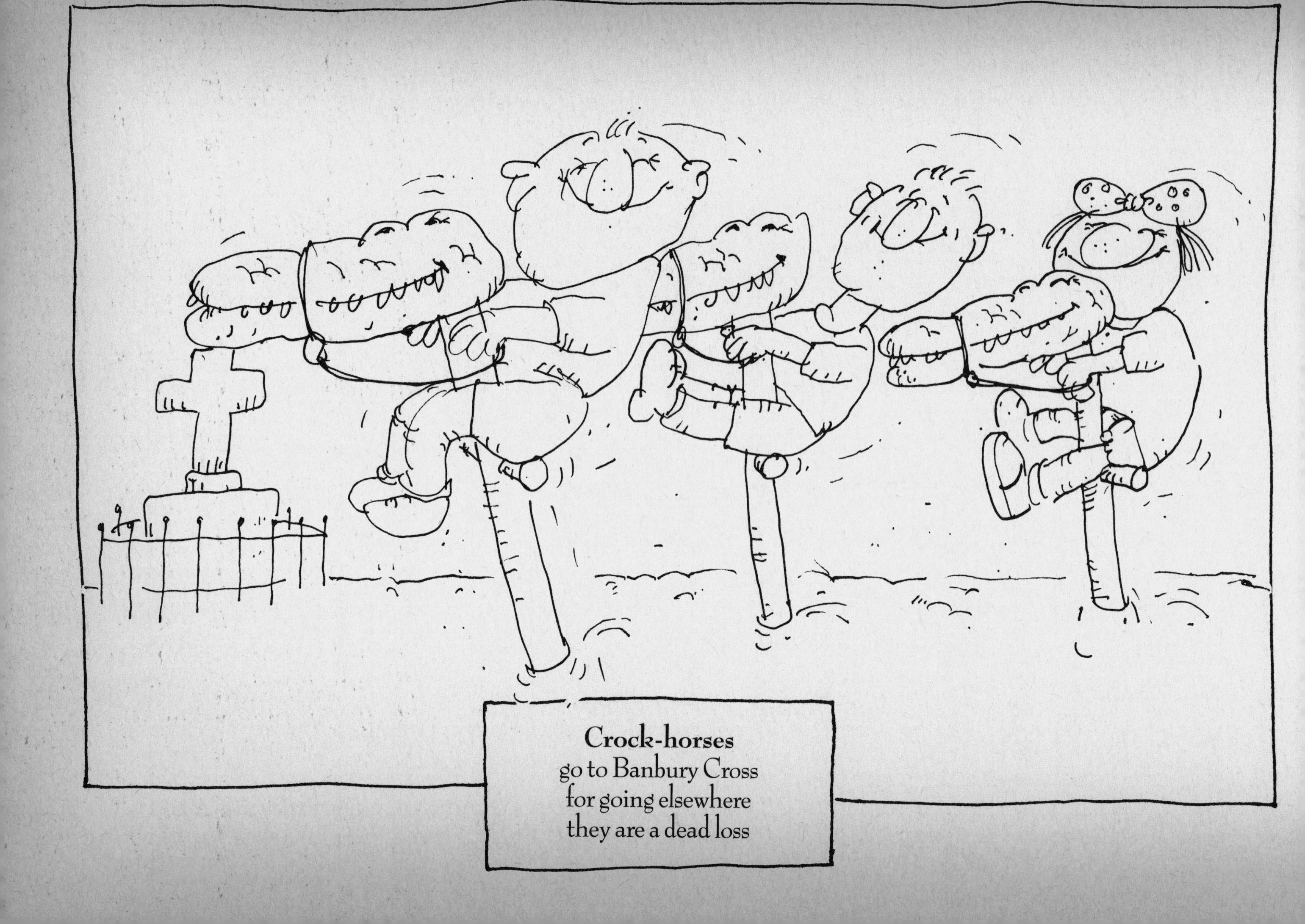

Crock-horses
go to Banbury Cross
for going elsewhere
they are a dead loss

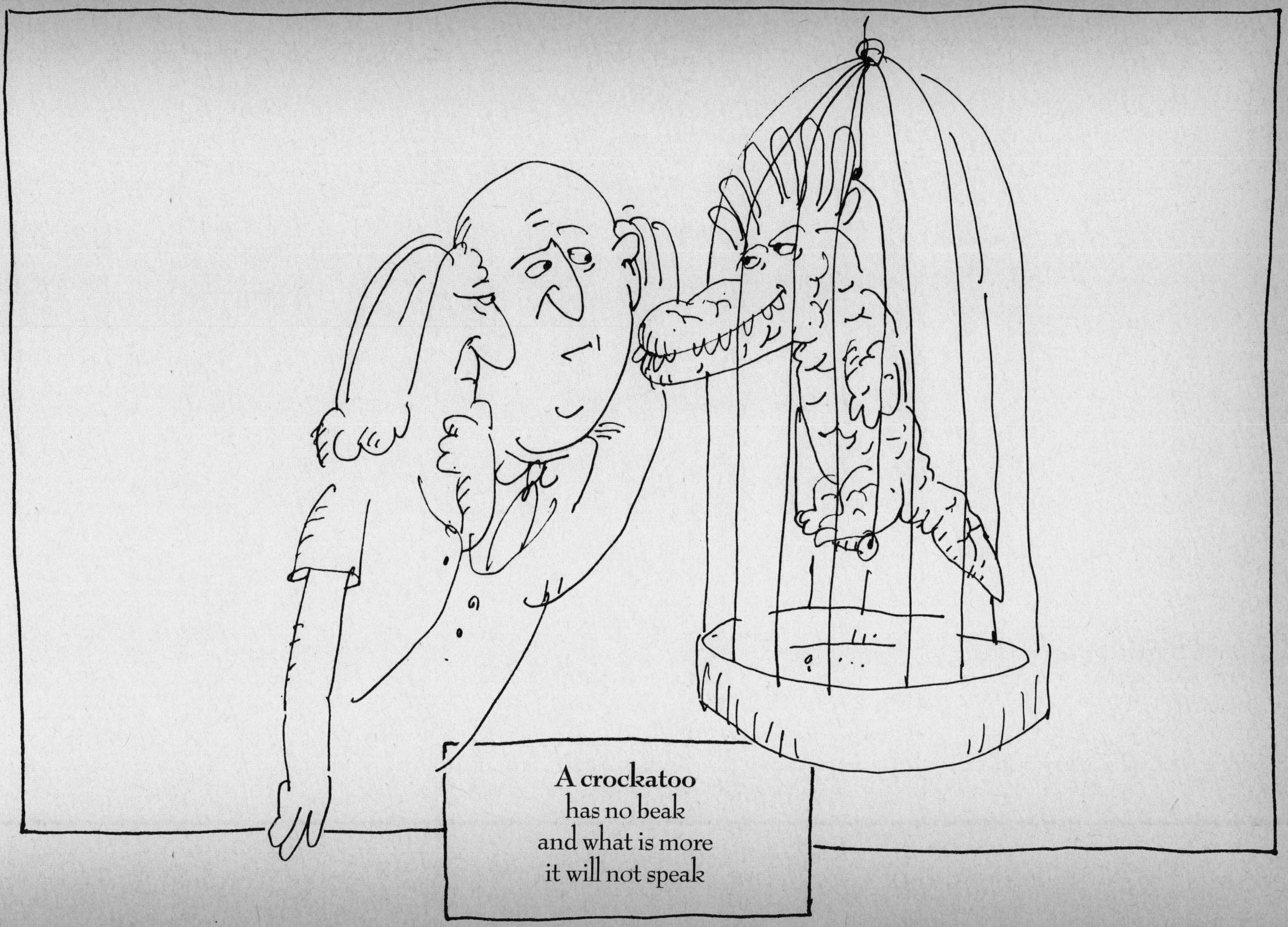

A crockatoo
has no beak
and what is more
it will not speak

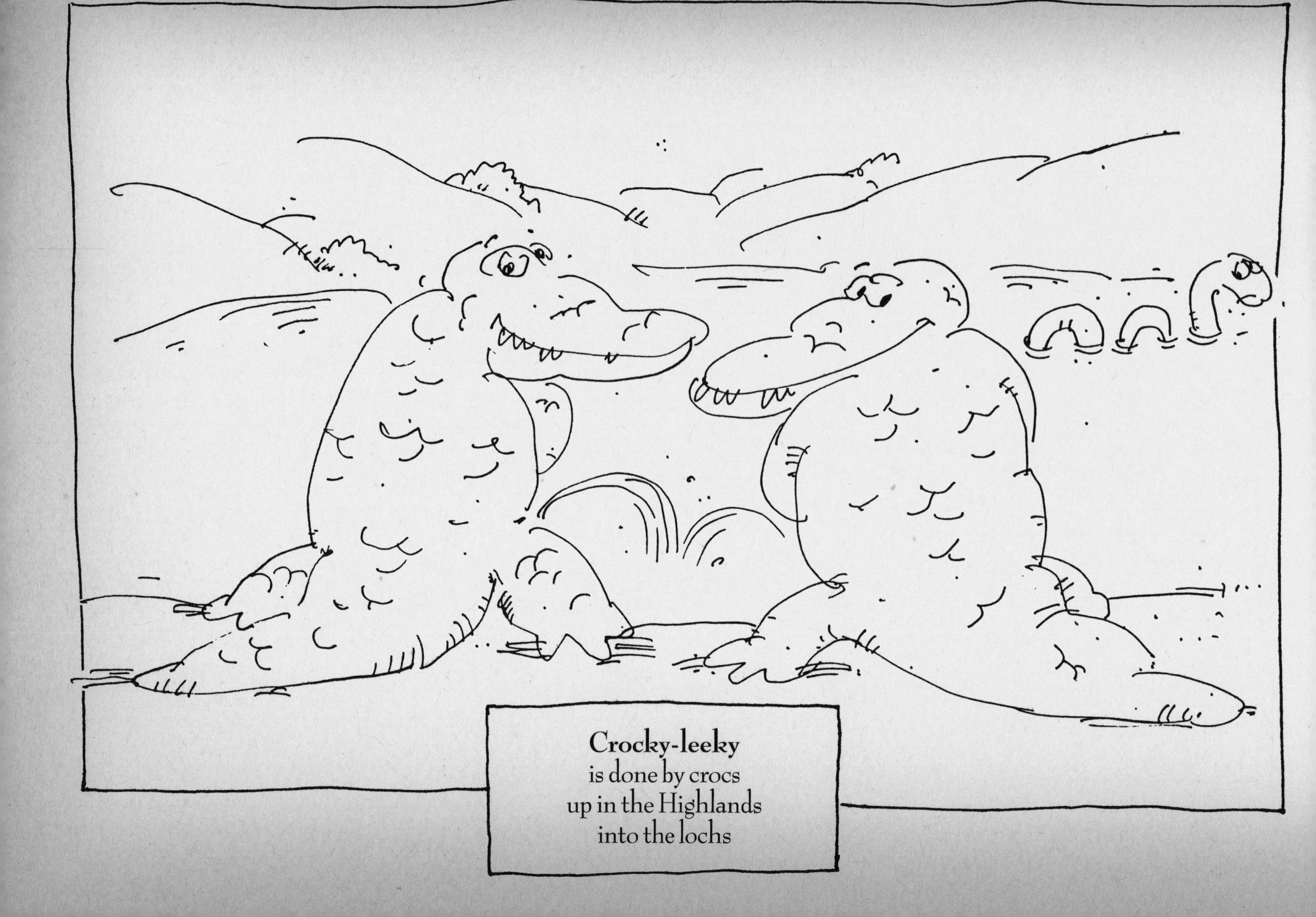

Crocky-leeky
is done by crocs
up in the Highlands
into the lochs

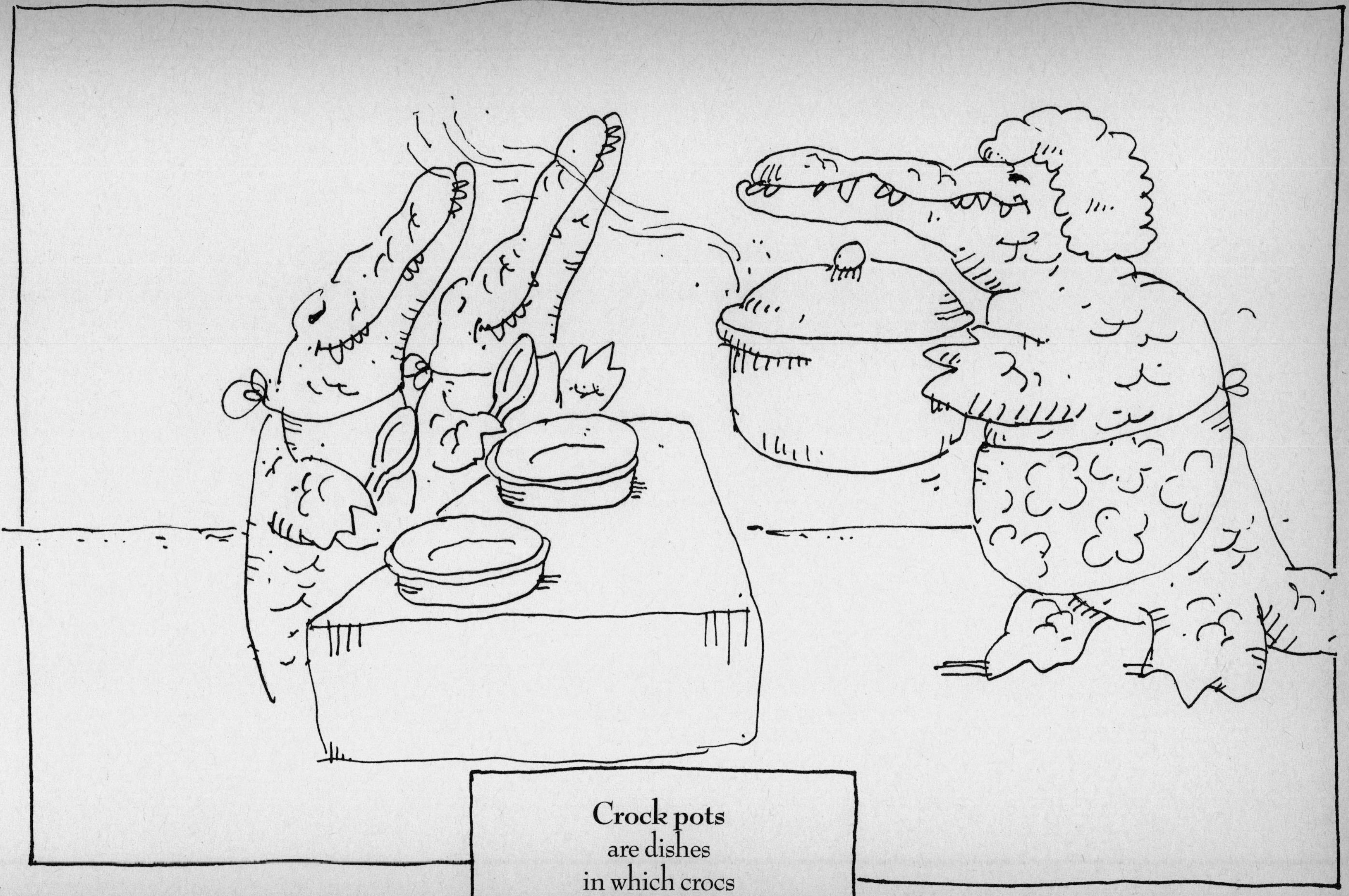

Crock pots
are dishes
in which crocs
cook their fishes

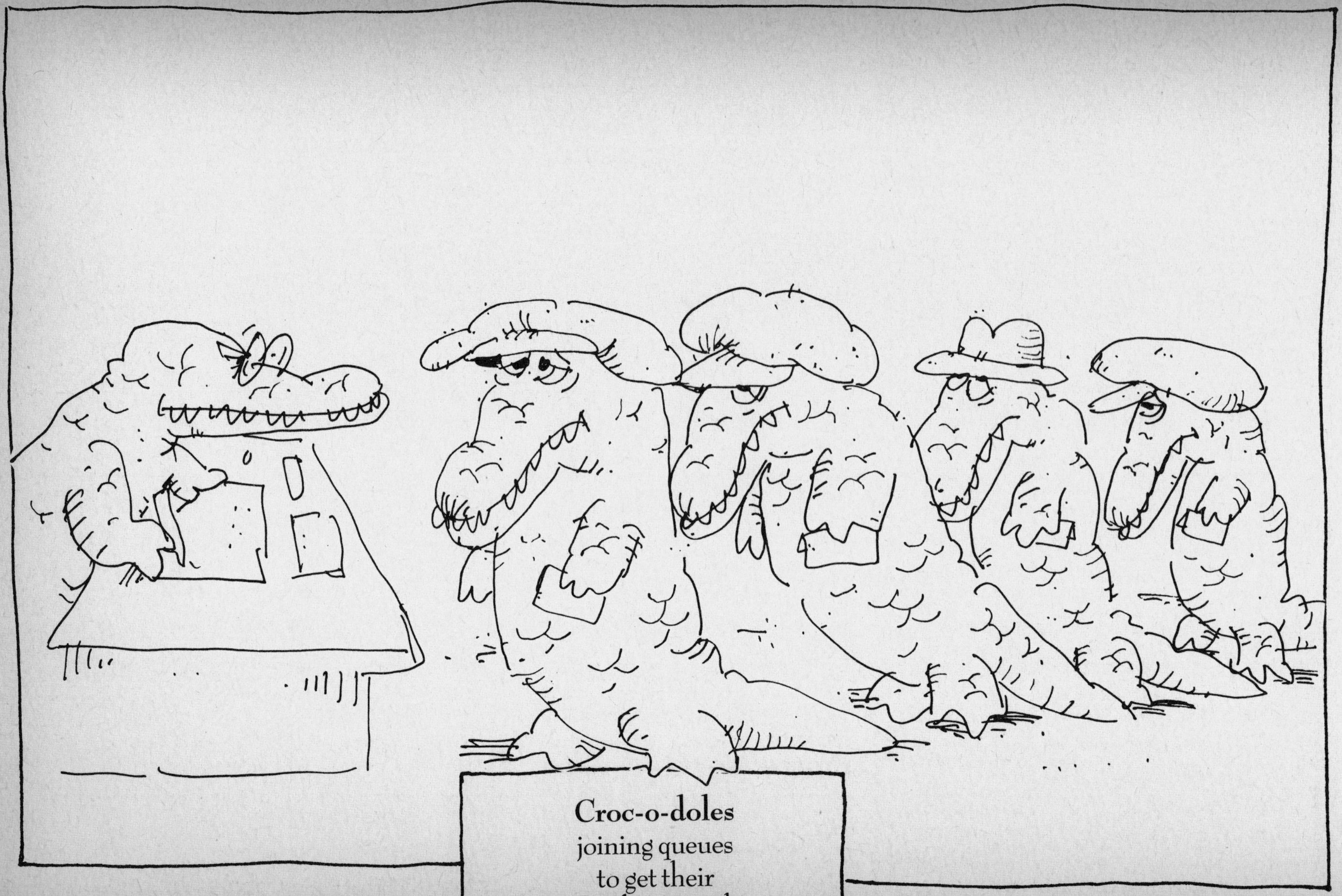

Croc-o-doles
joining queues
to get their
unemployment dues

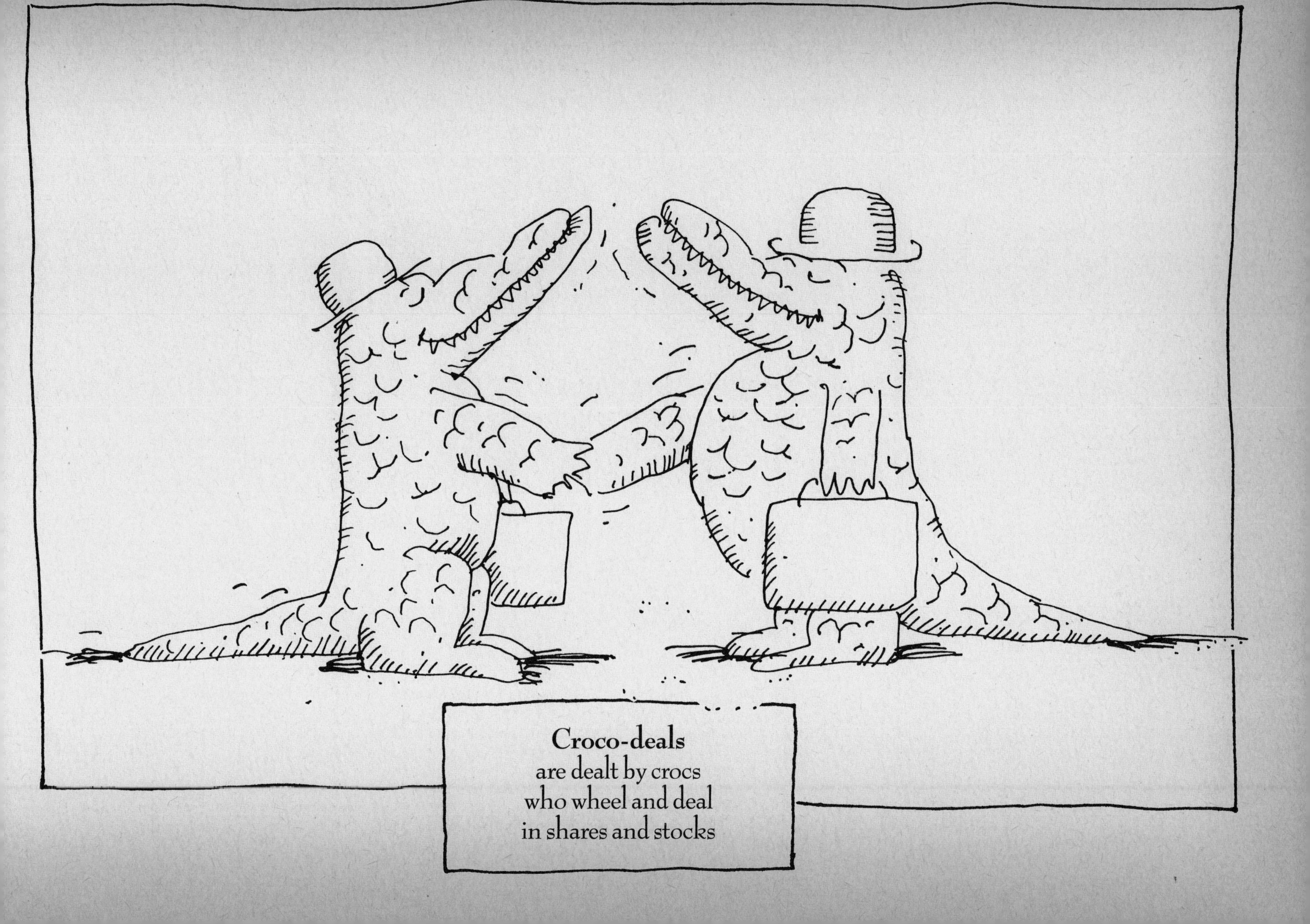

Croco-deals
are dealt by crocs
who wheel and deal
in shares and stocks

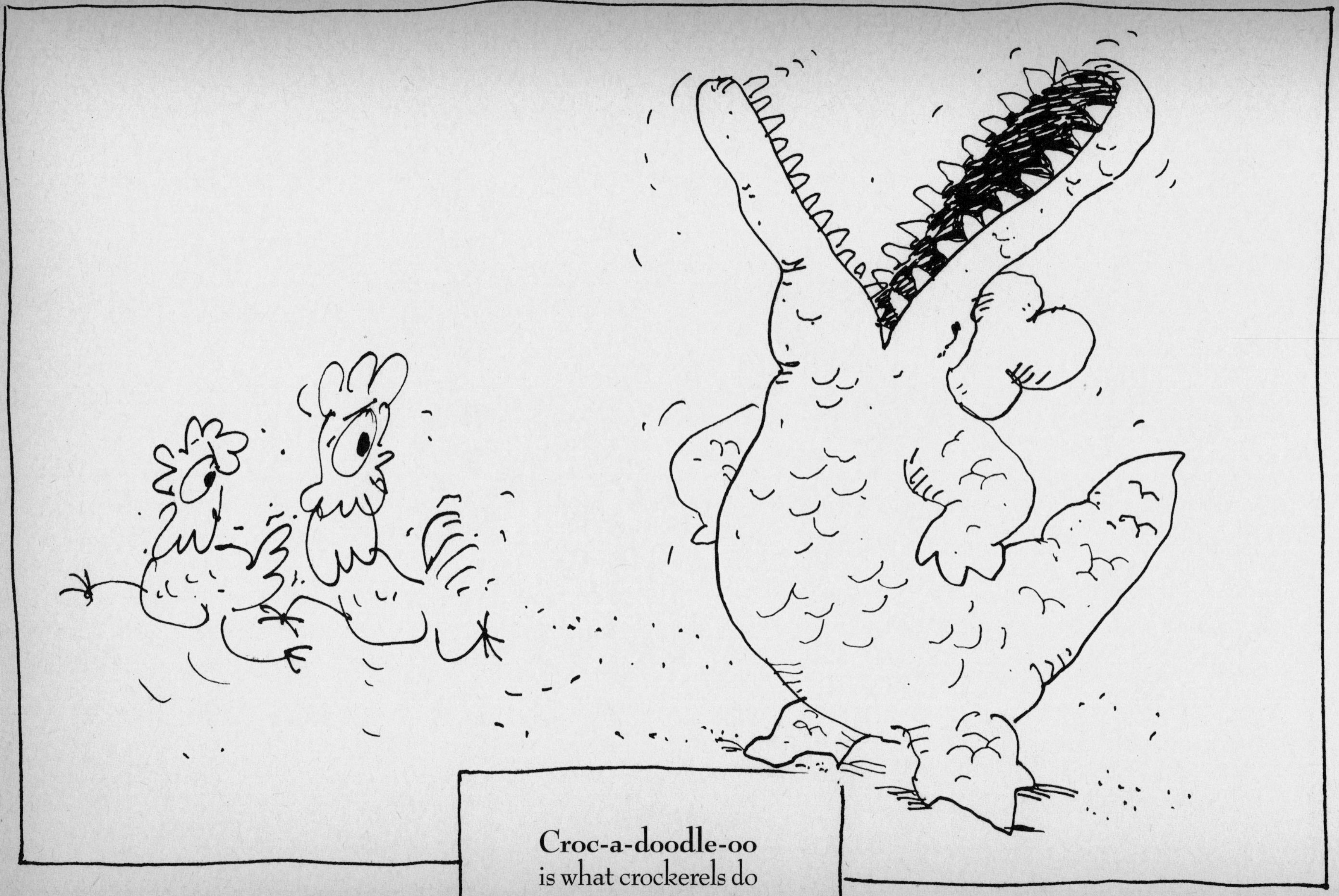

Croc-a-doodle-oo
is what crockerels do

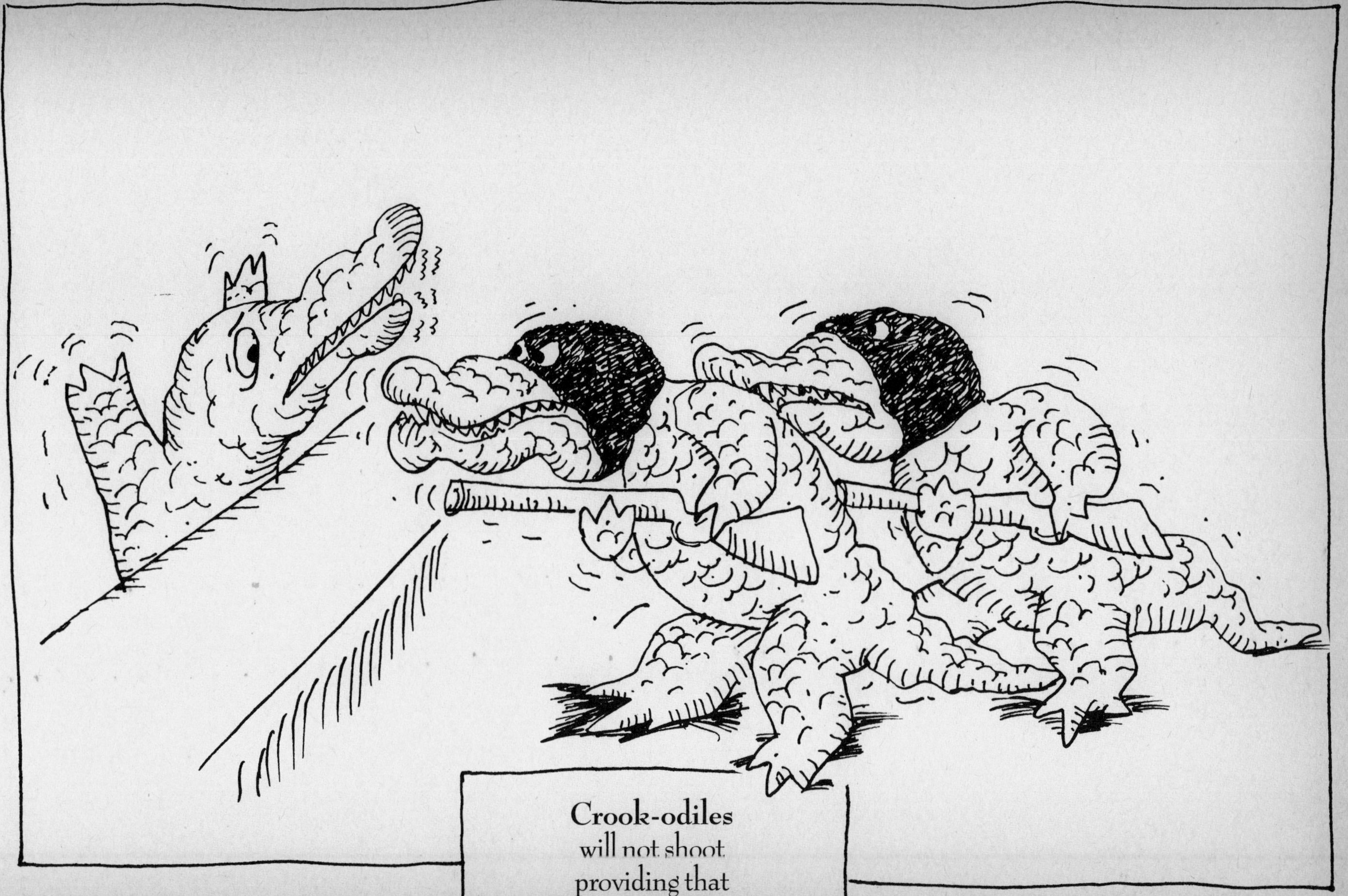

Crook-odiles
will not shoot
providing that
they get the loot

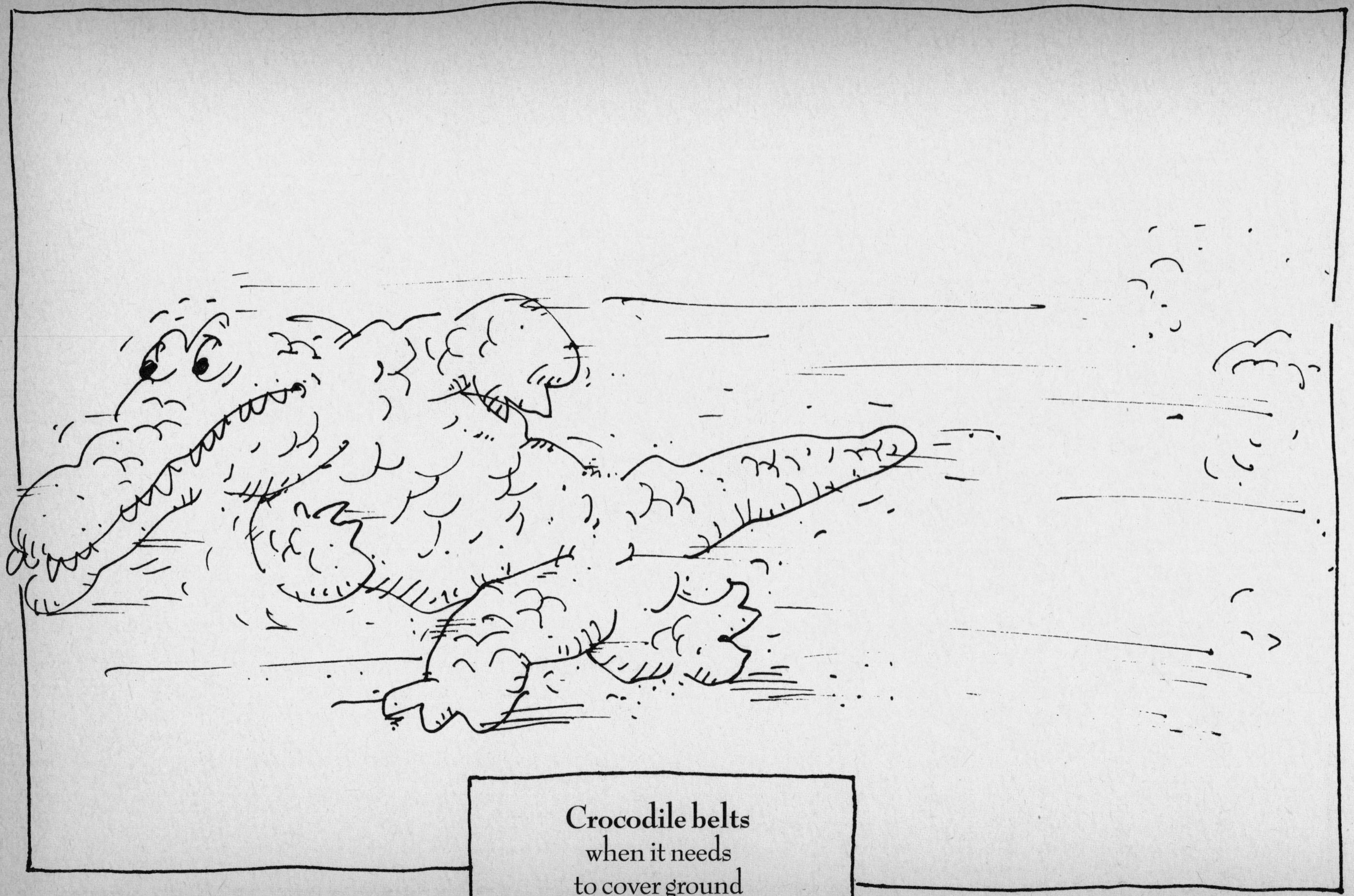

Crocodile belts
when it needs
to cover ground
at rapid speeds

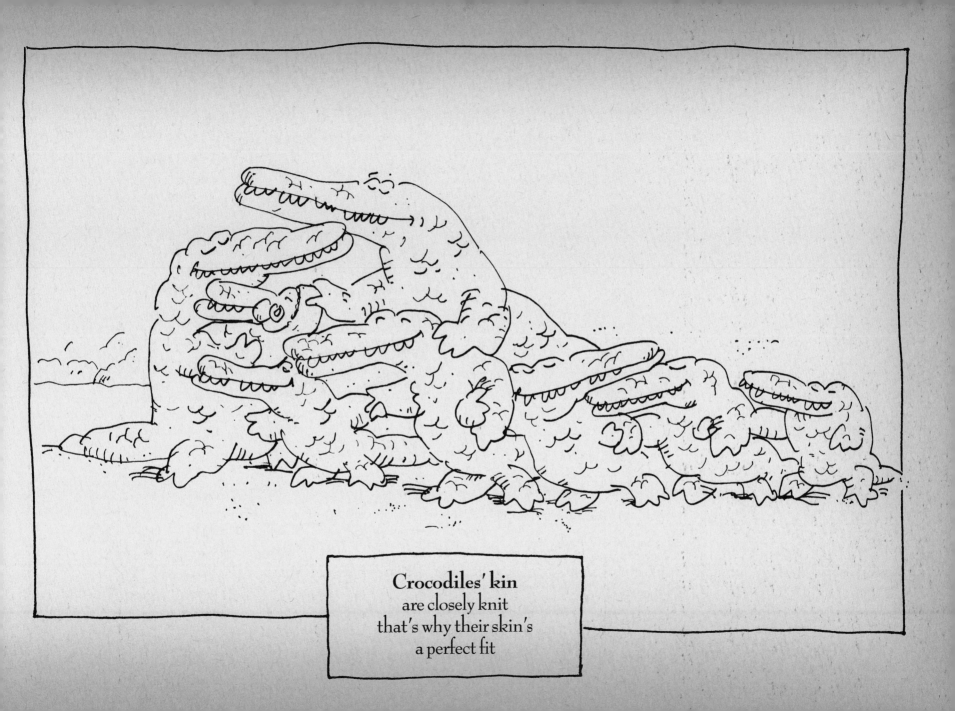

Crocodiles' kin
are closely knit
that's why their skin's
a perfect fit

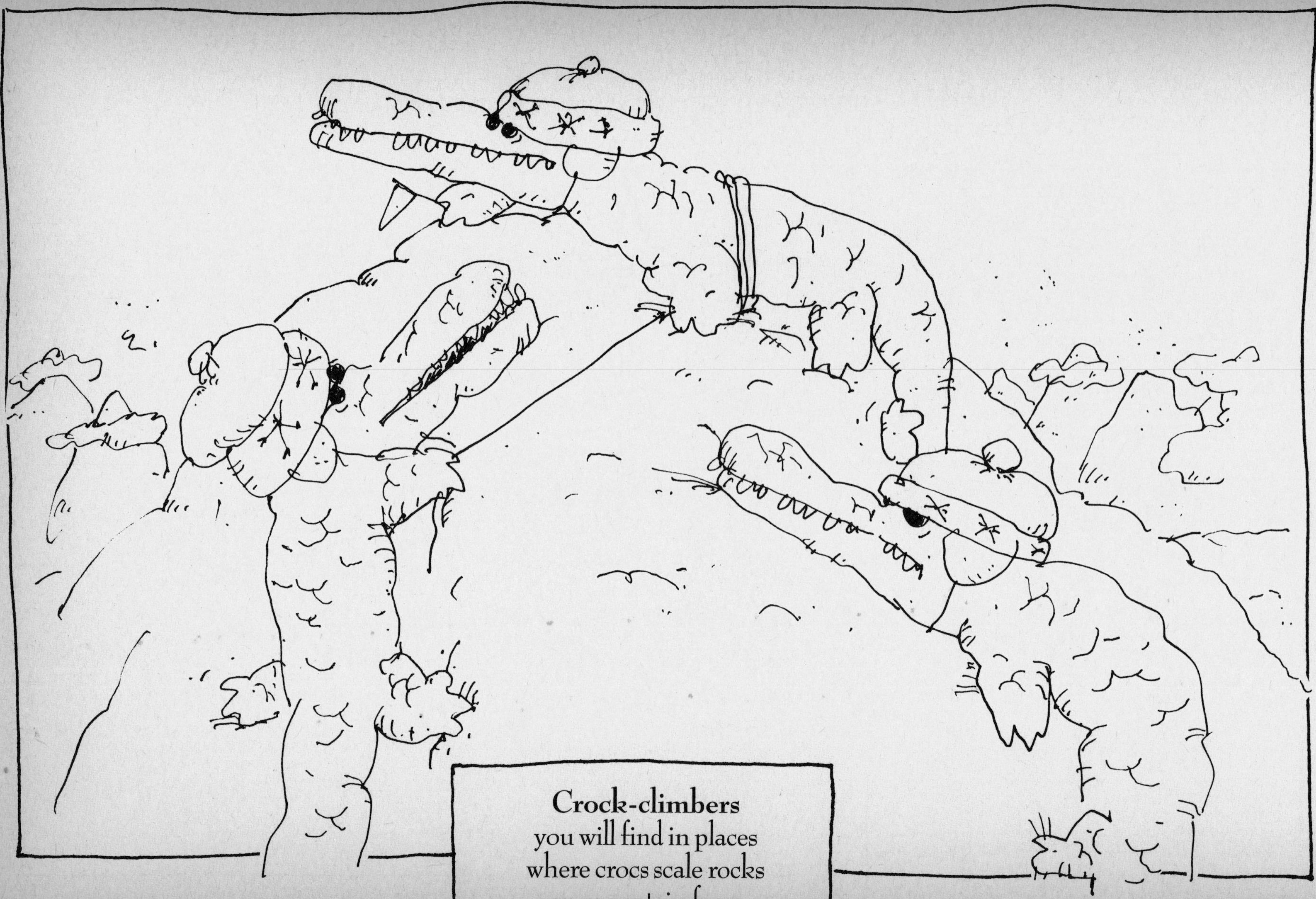

Crock-climbers
you will find in places
where crocs scale rocks
on mountain faces

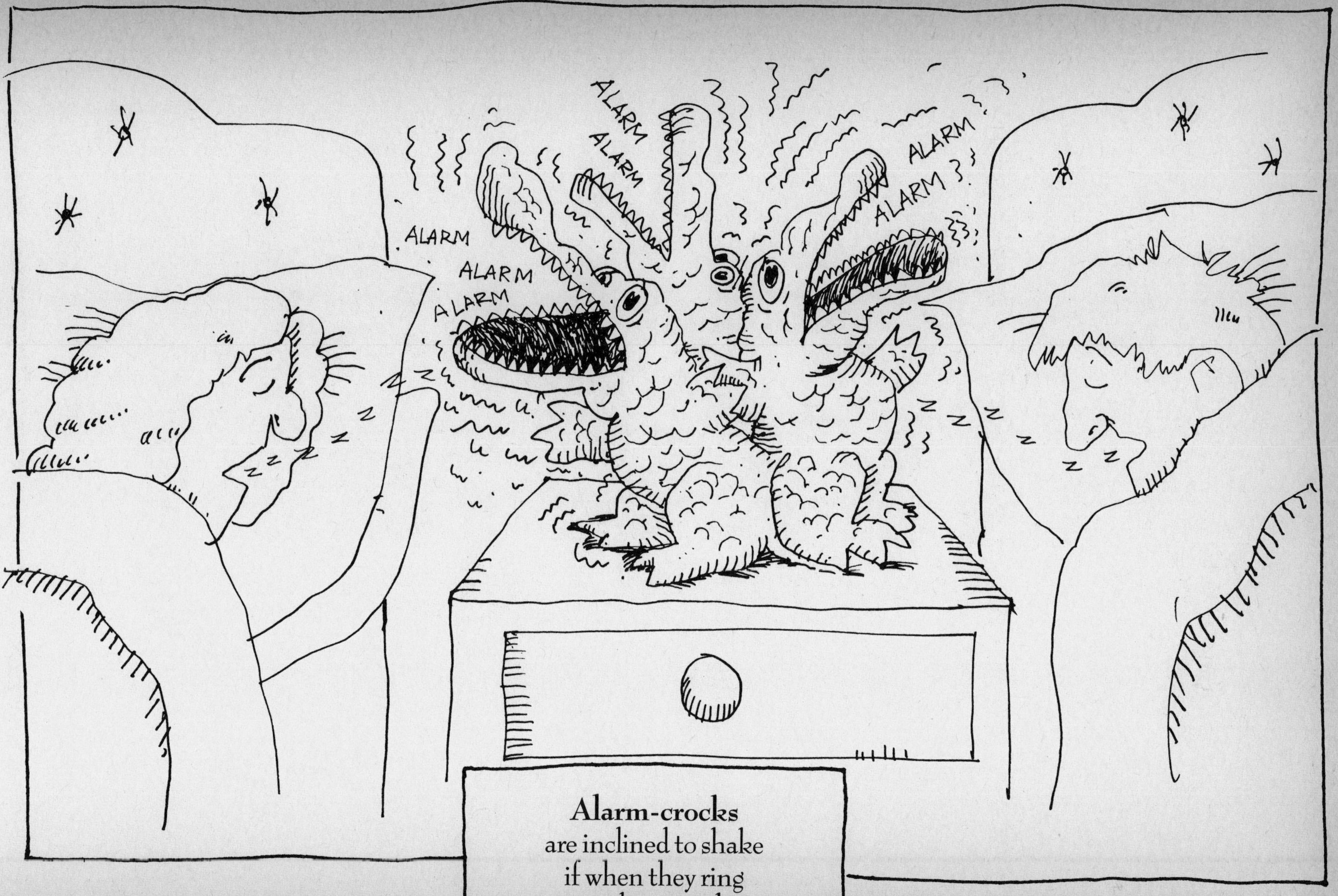
ALARM
ALARM
ALARM
ALARM
ALARM
ALARM
ALARM
ALARM
ALARM

Alarm-crocks
are inclined to shake
if when they ring
you do not wake

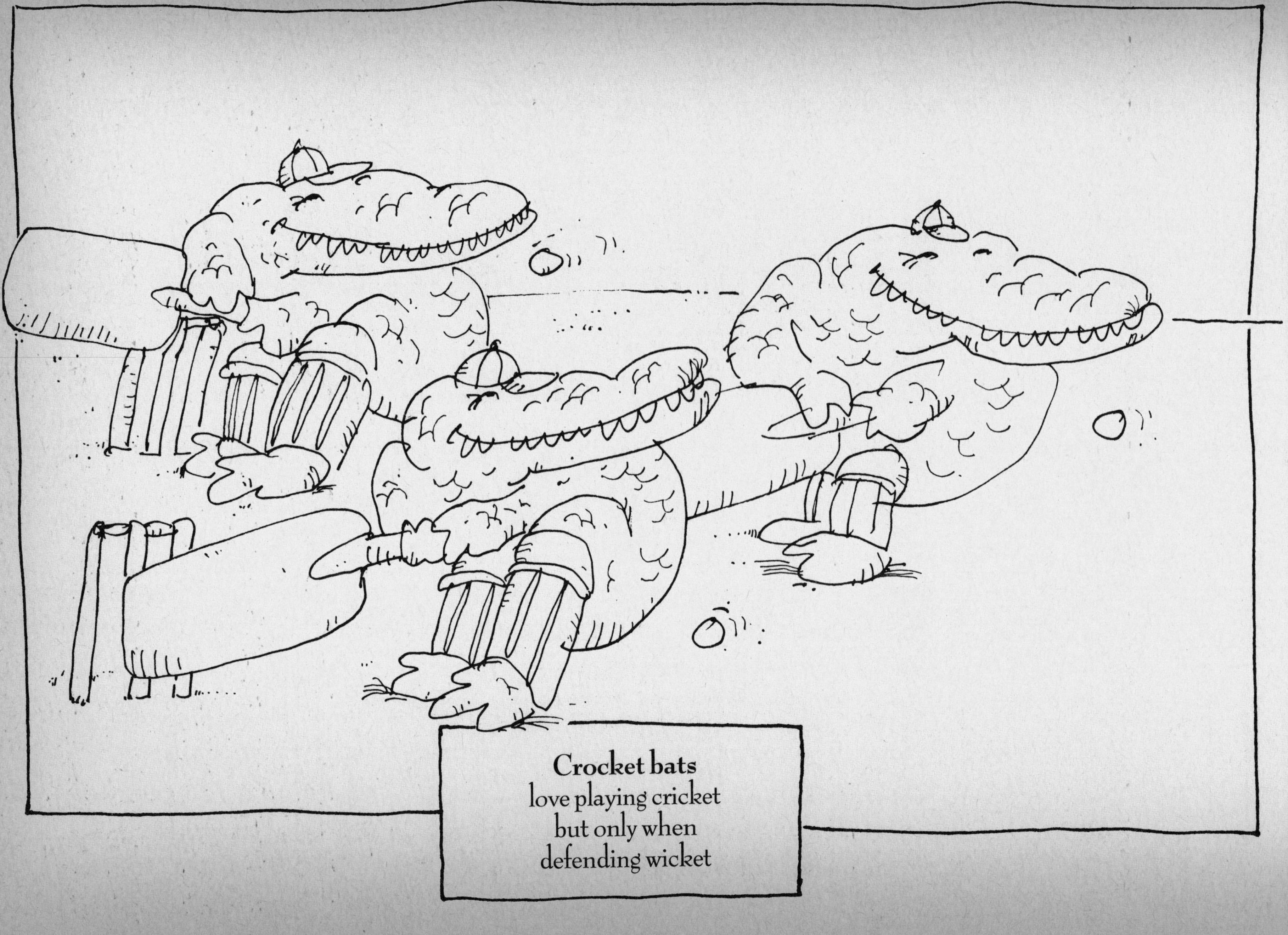

Crocket bats
love playing cricket
but only when
defending wicket

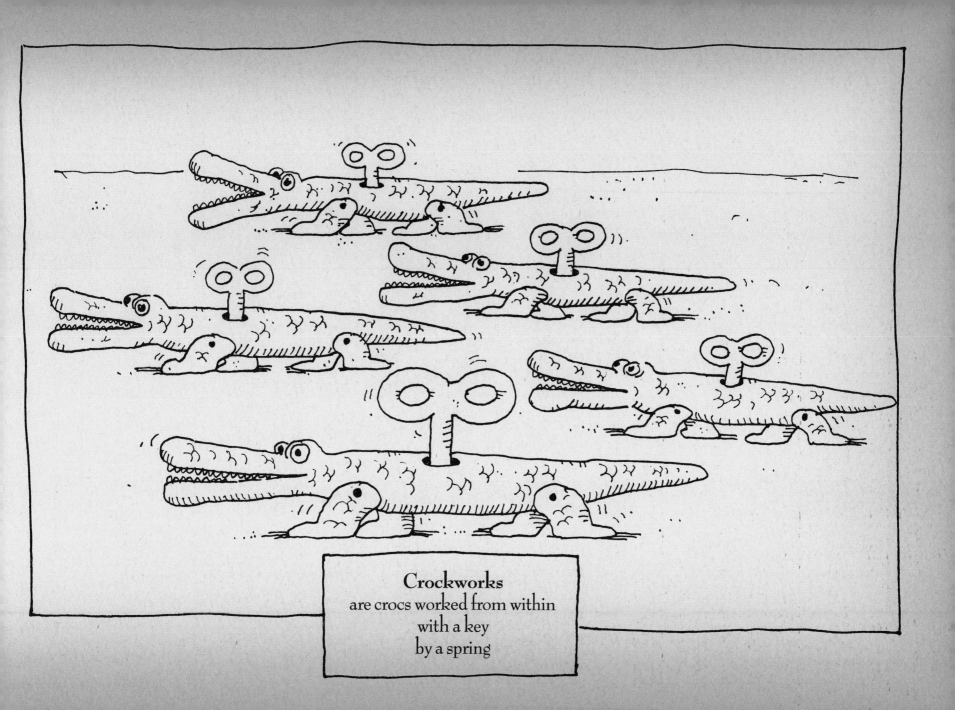

Crockworks
are crocs worked from within
with a key
by a spring

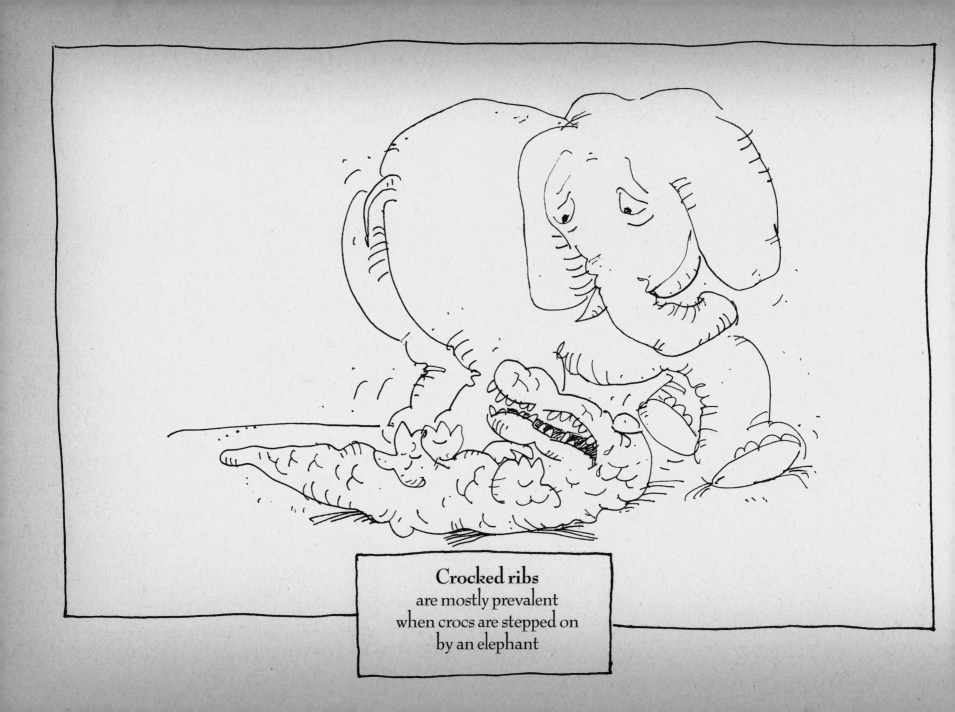

Crocked ribs
are mostly prevalent
when crocs are stepped on
by an elephant

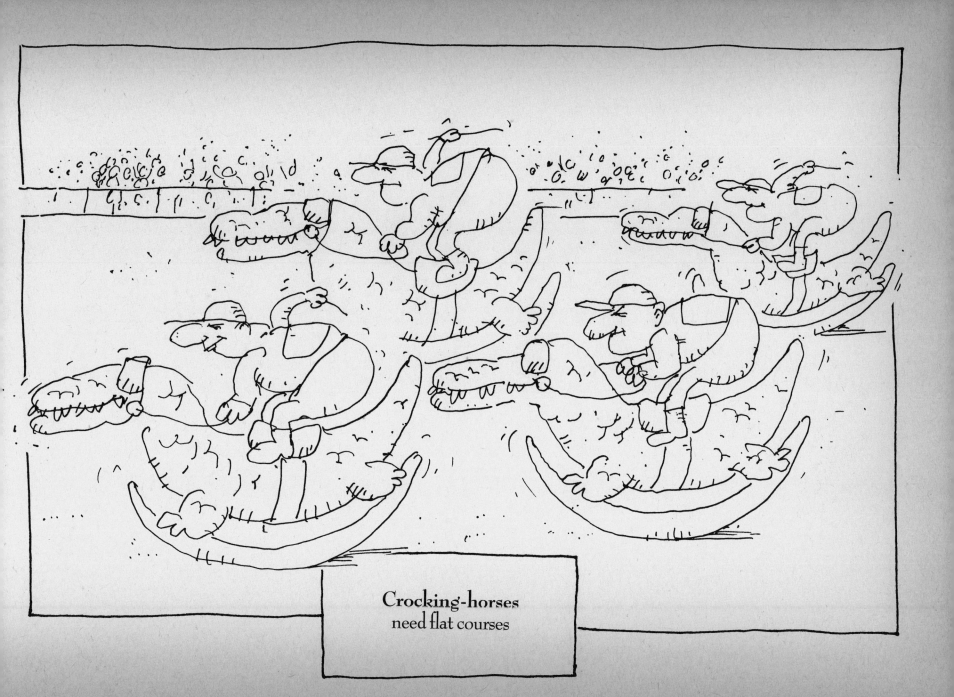

Crocking-horses
need flat courses

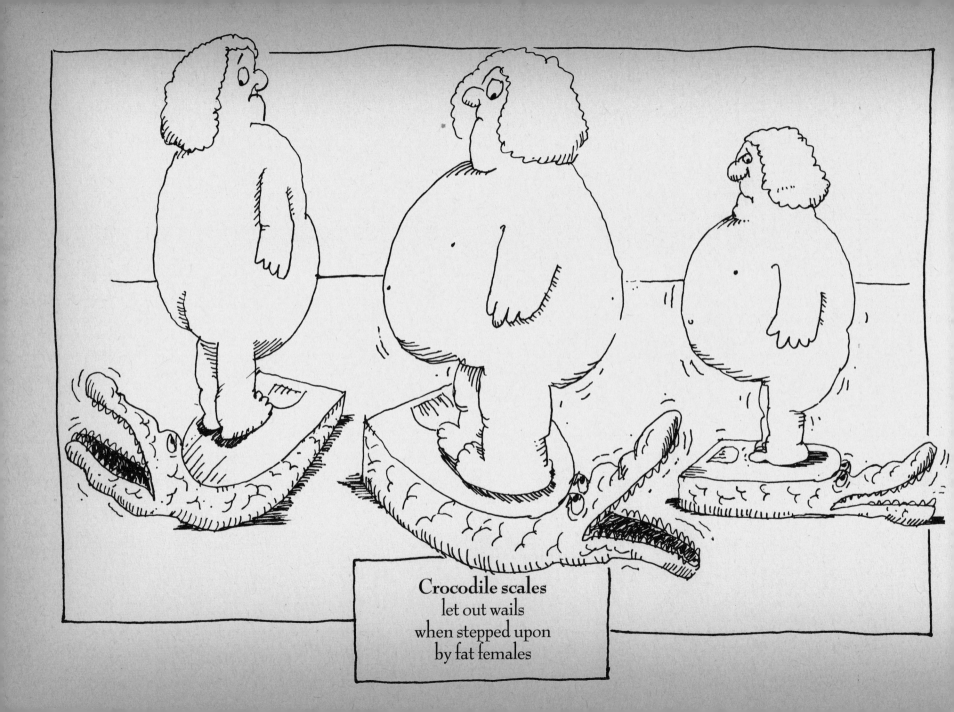

Crocodile scales
let out wails
when stepped upon
by fat females

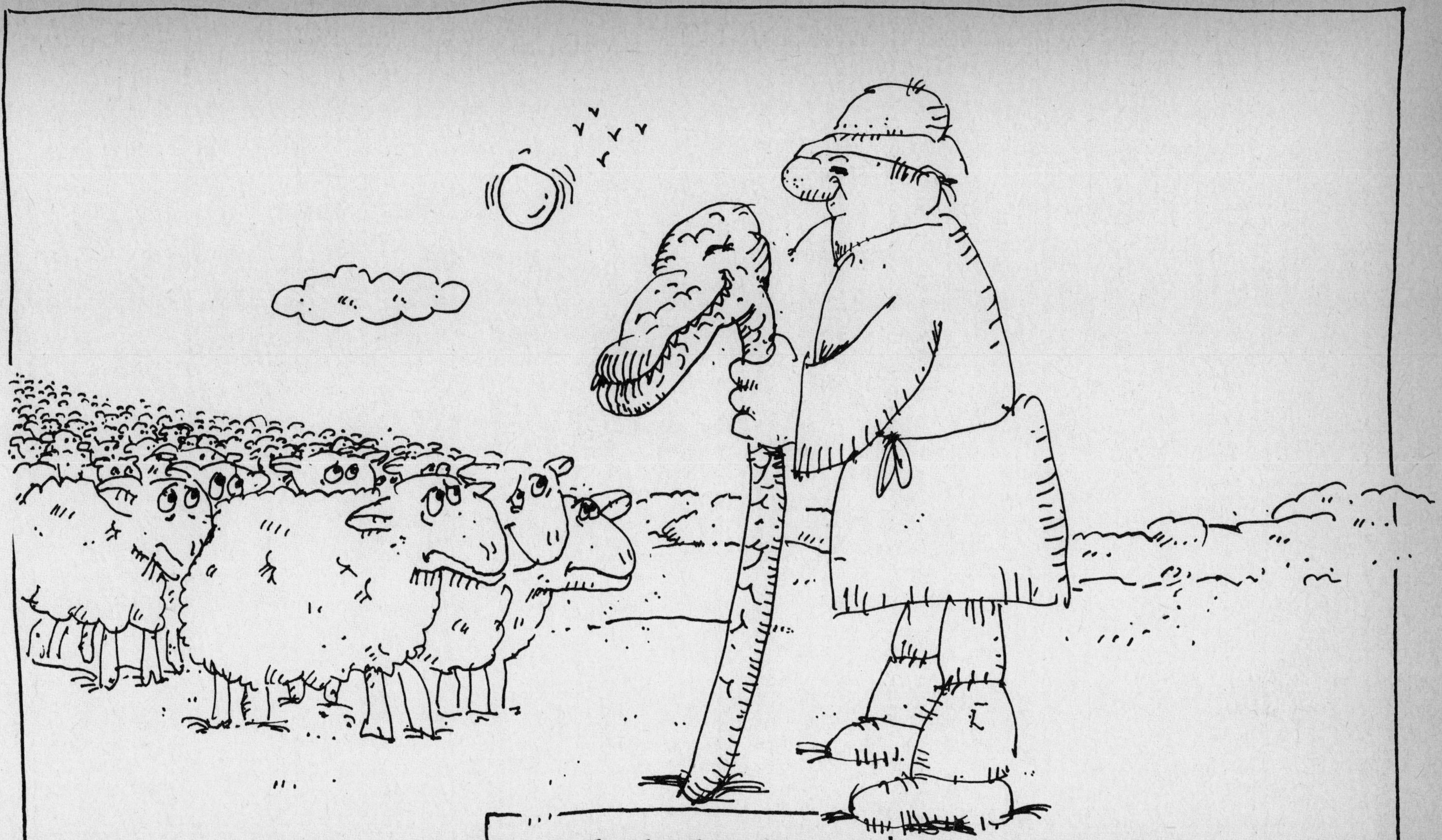

Shepherds' crocks
are held in hands
of shepherds tending
sheep and lambs

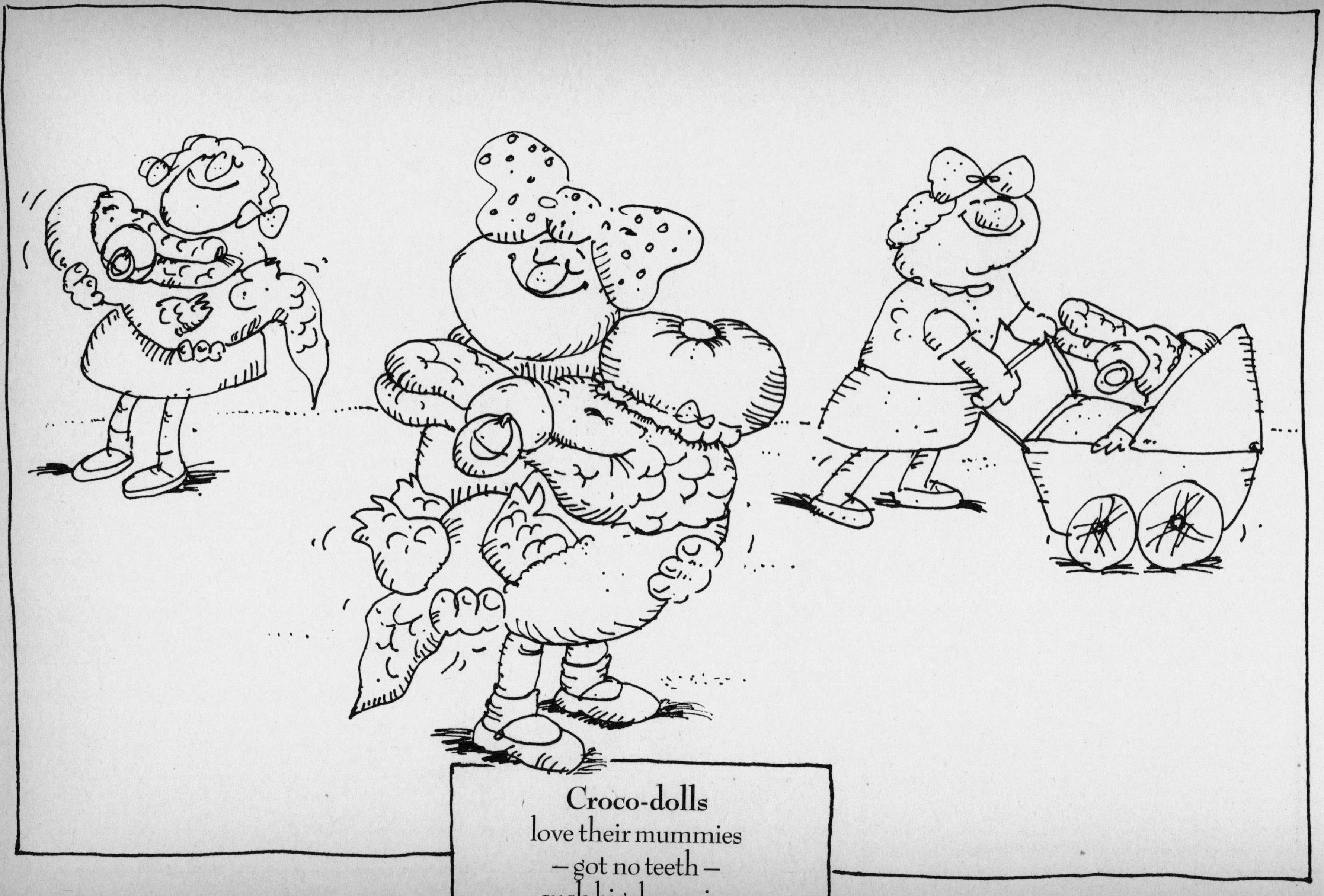

Croco-dolls
love their mummies
– got no teeth –
suck big dummies

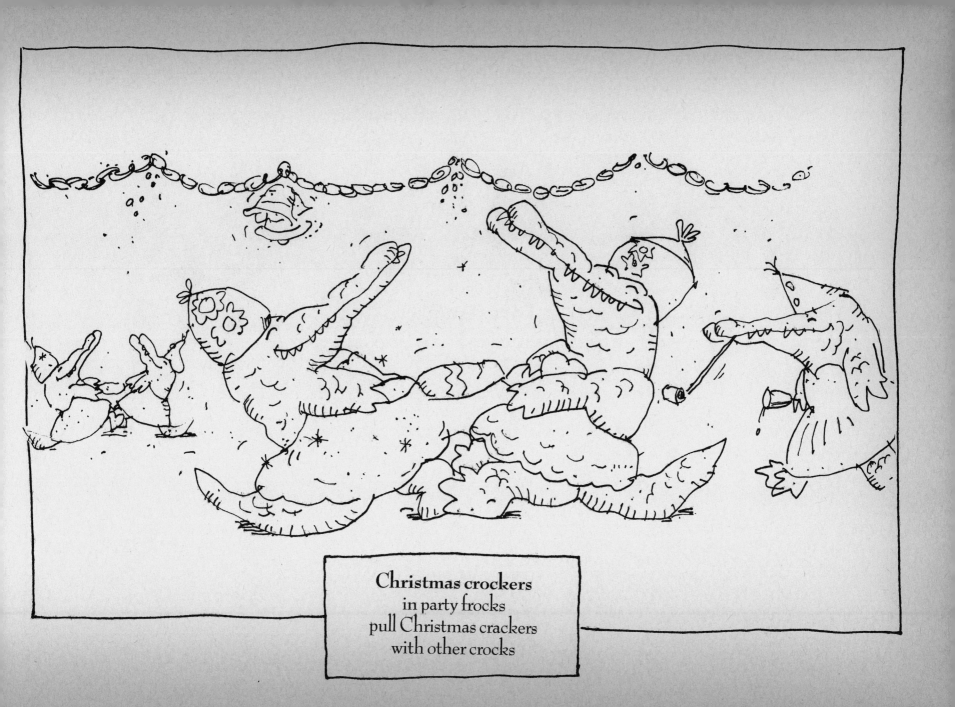

Christmas crockers
in party frocks
pull Christmas crackers
with other crocks

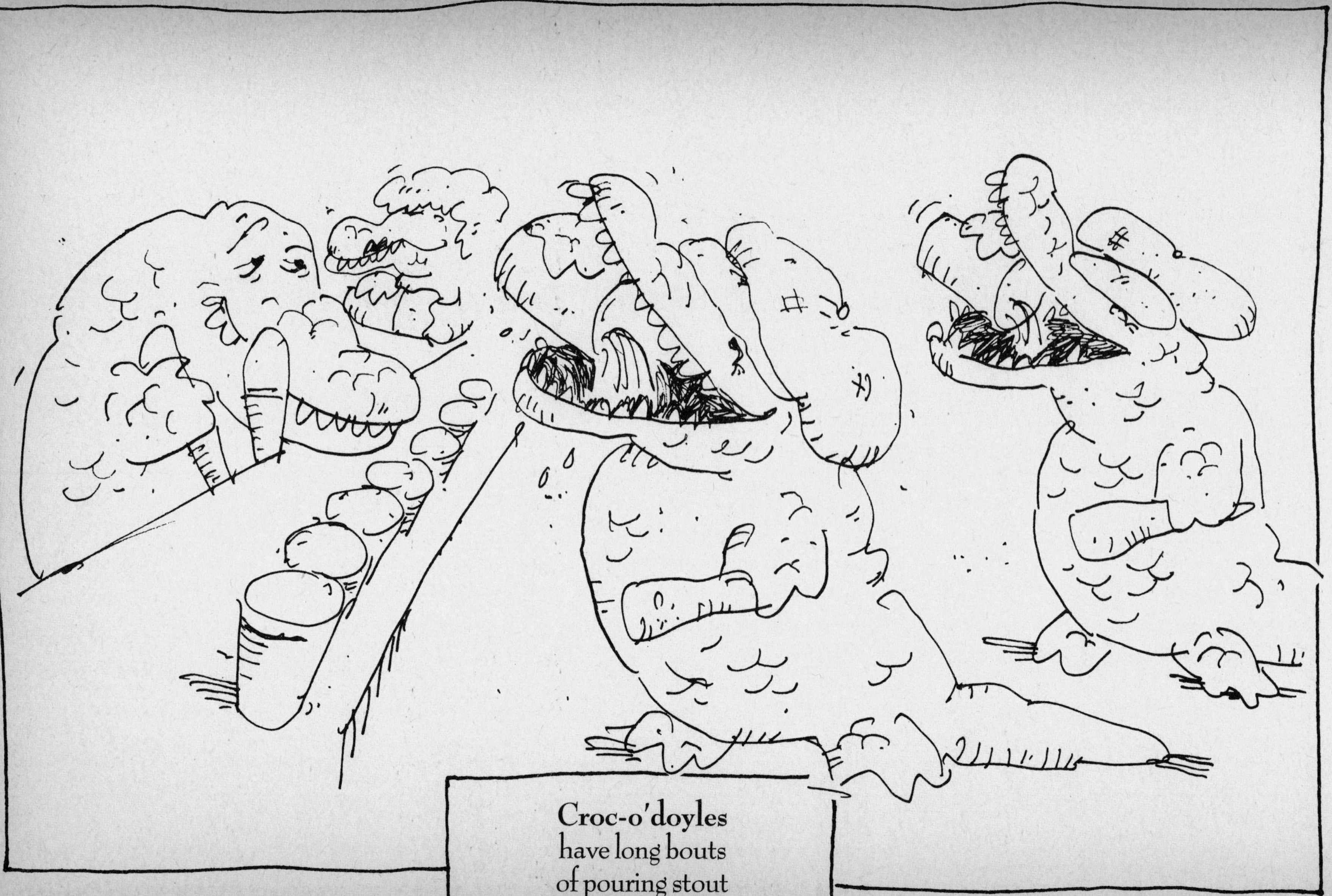

Croc-o'doyles
have long bouts
of pouring stout
down their snouts

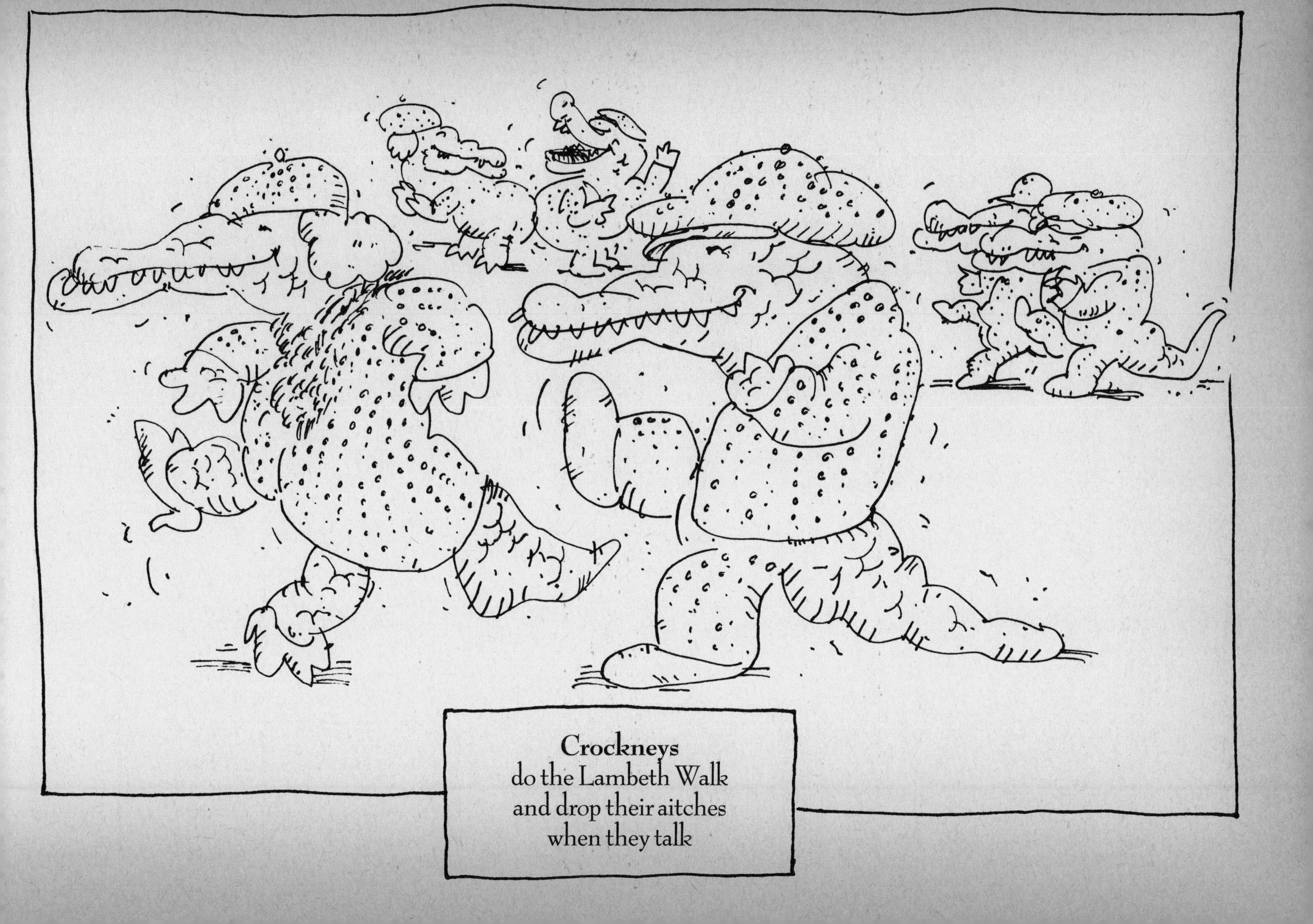

Crockneys
do the Lambeth Walk
and drop their aitches
when they talk

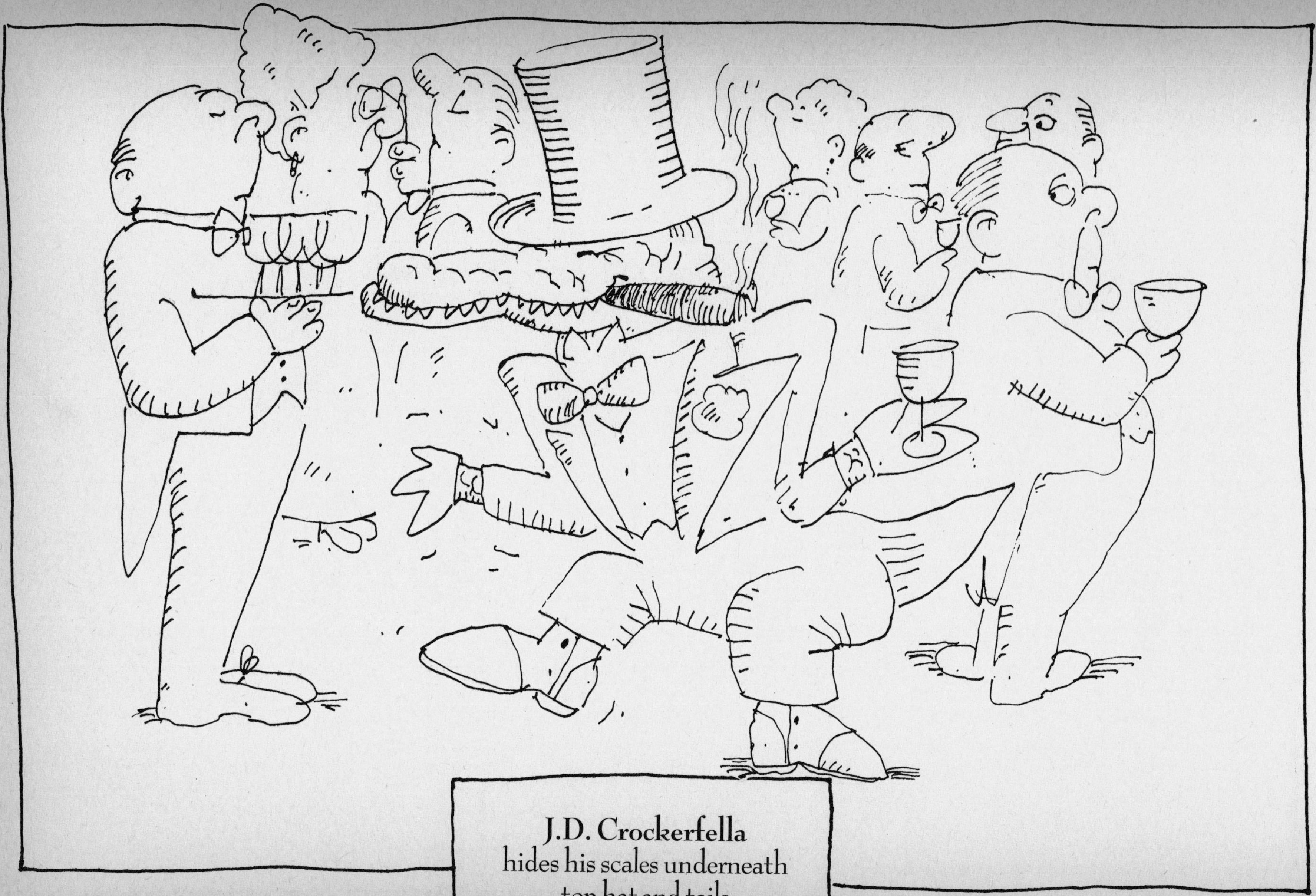

J.D. Crockerfella
hides his scales underneath
top hat and tails

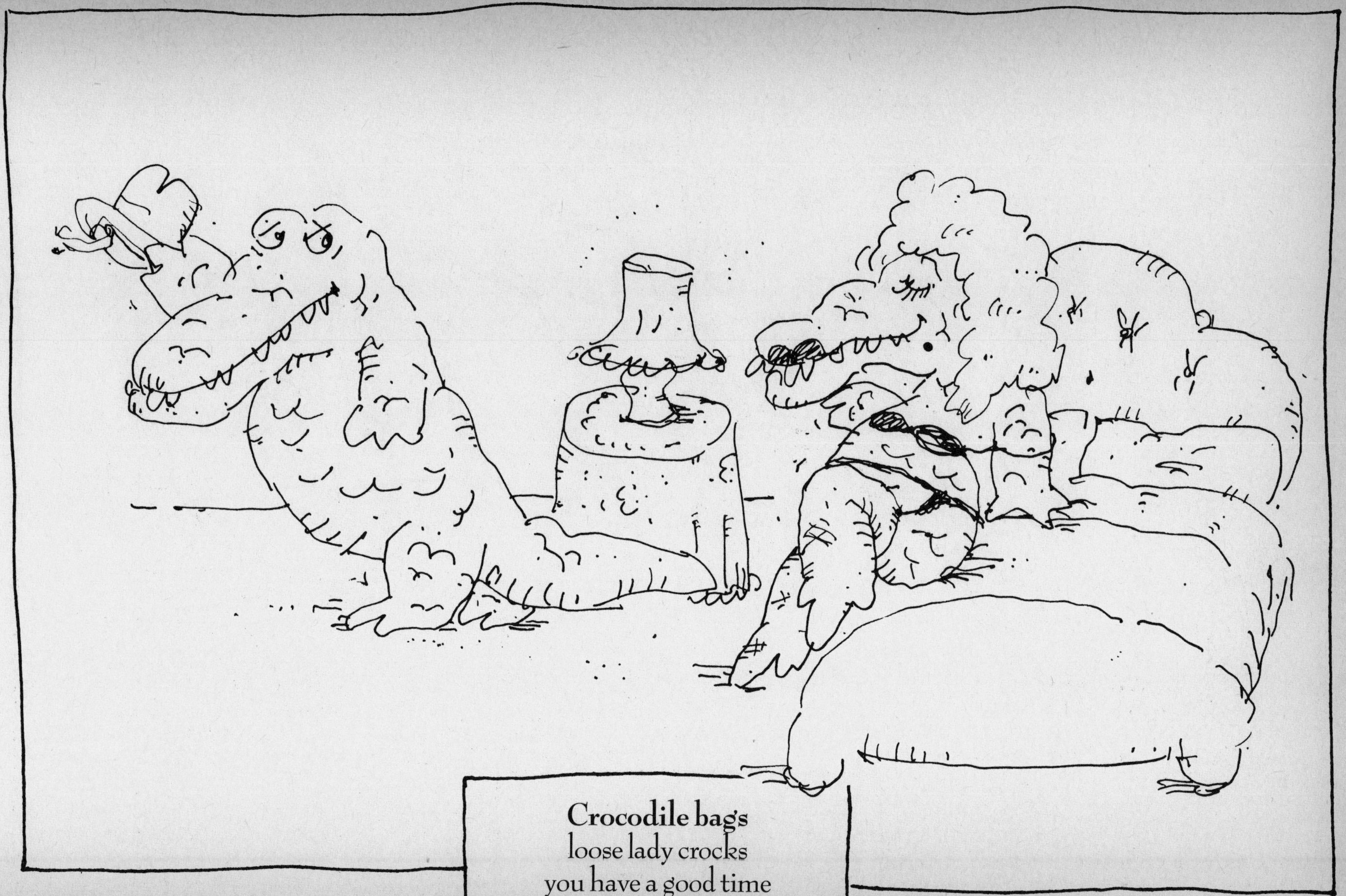

Crocodile bags
loose lady crocks
you have a good time
and you get the pox

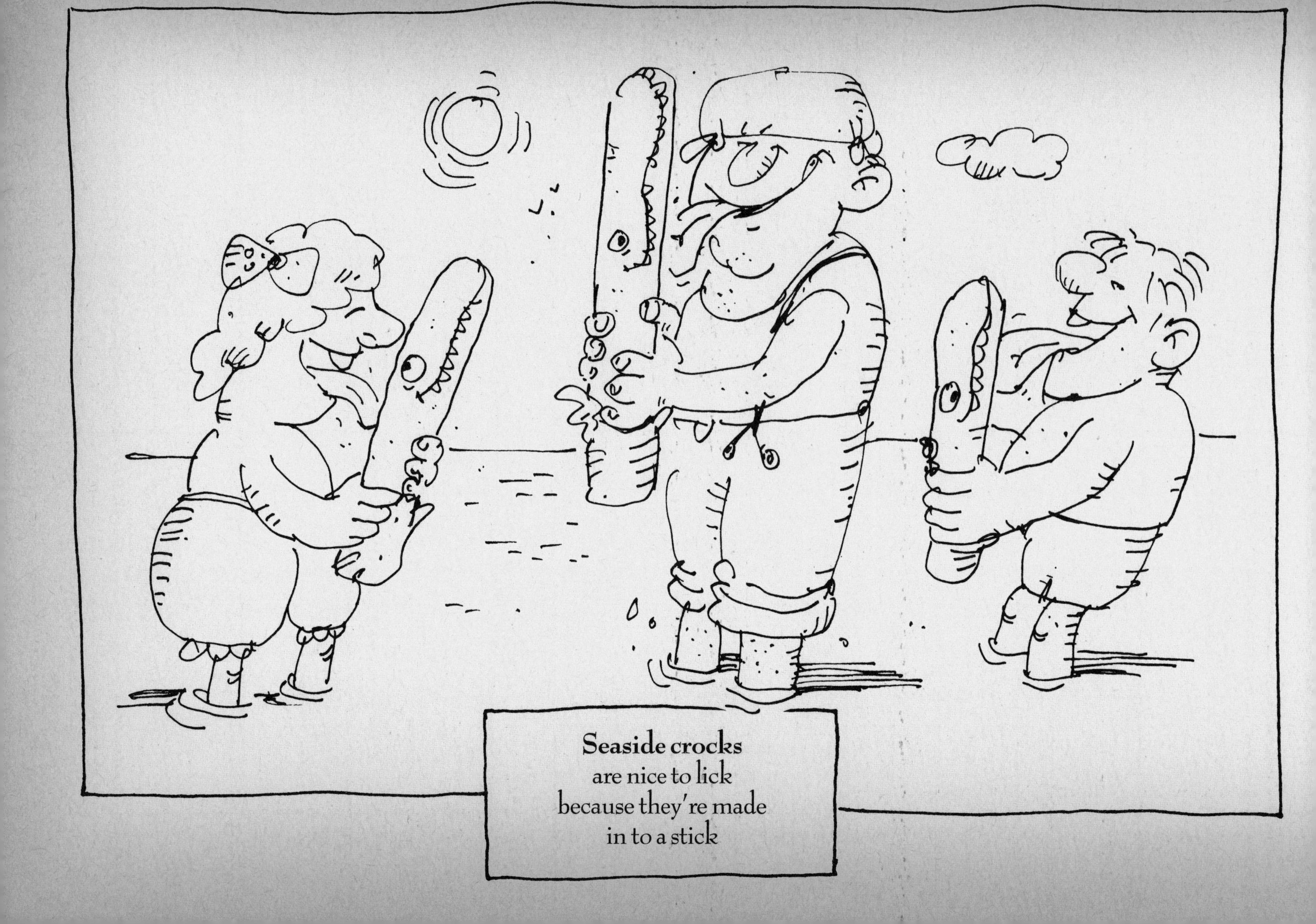

Seaside crocks
are nice to lick
because they're made
in to a stick

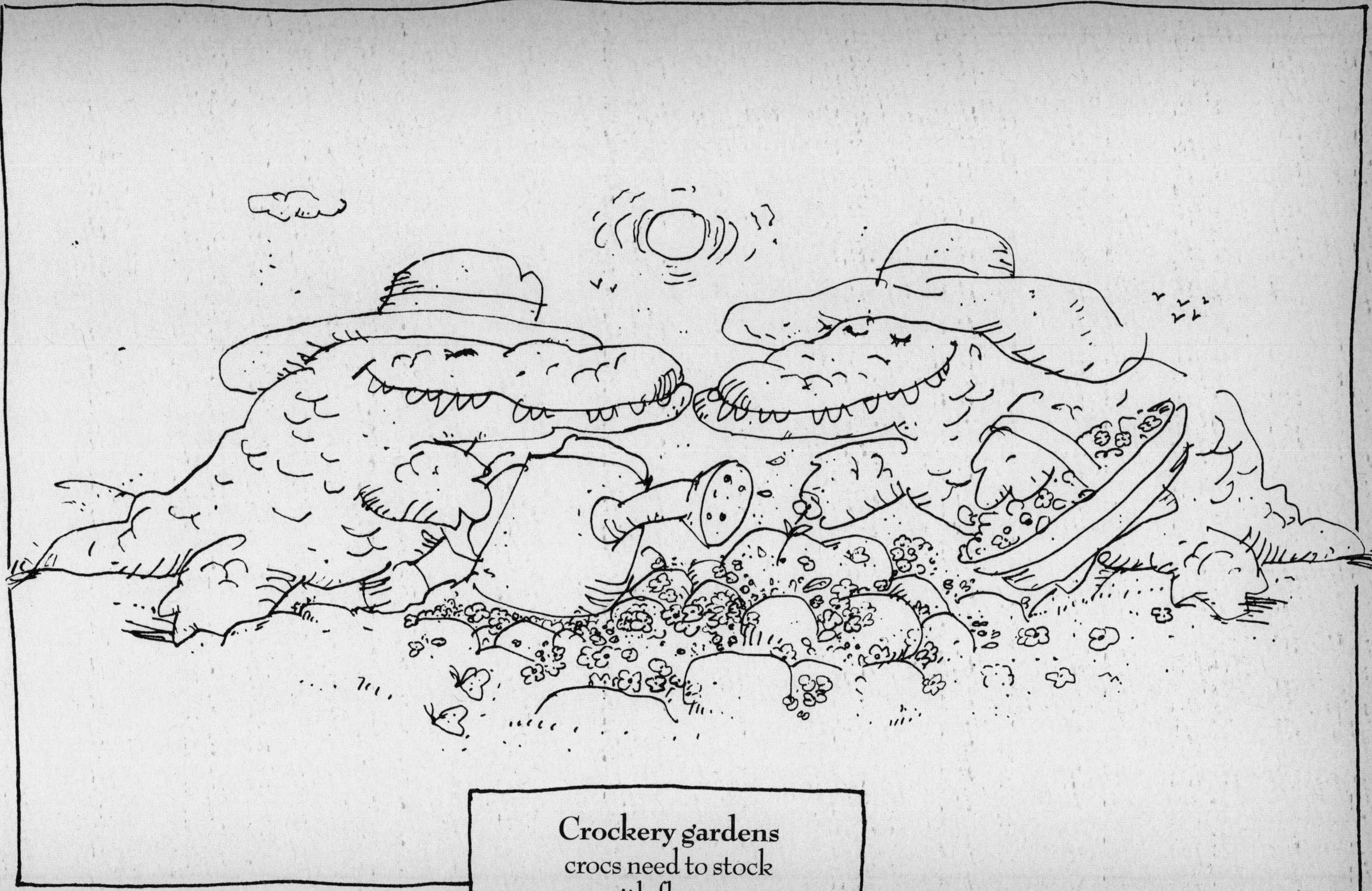

Crockery gardens
crocs need to stock
with flowers
that are fond of rocks

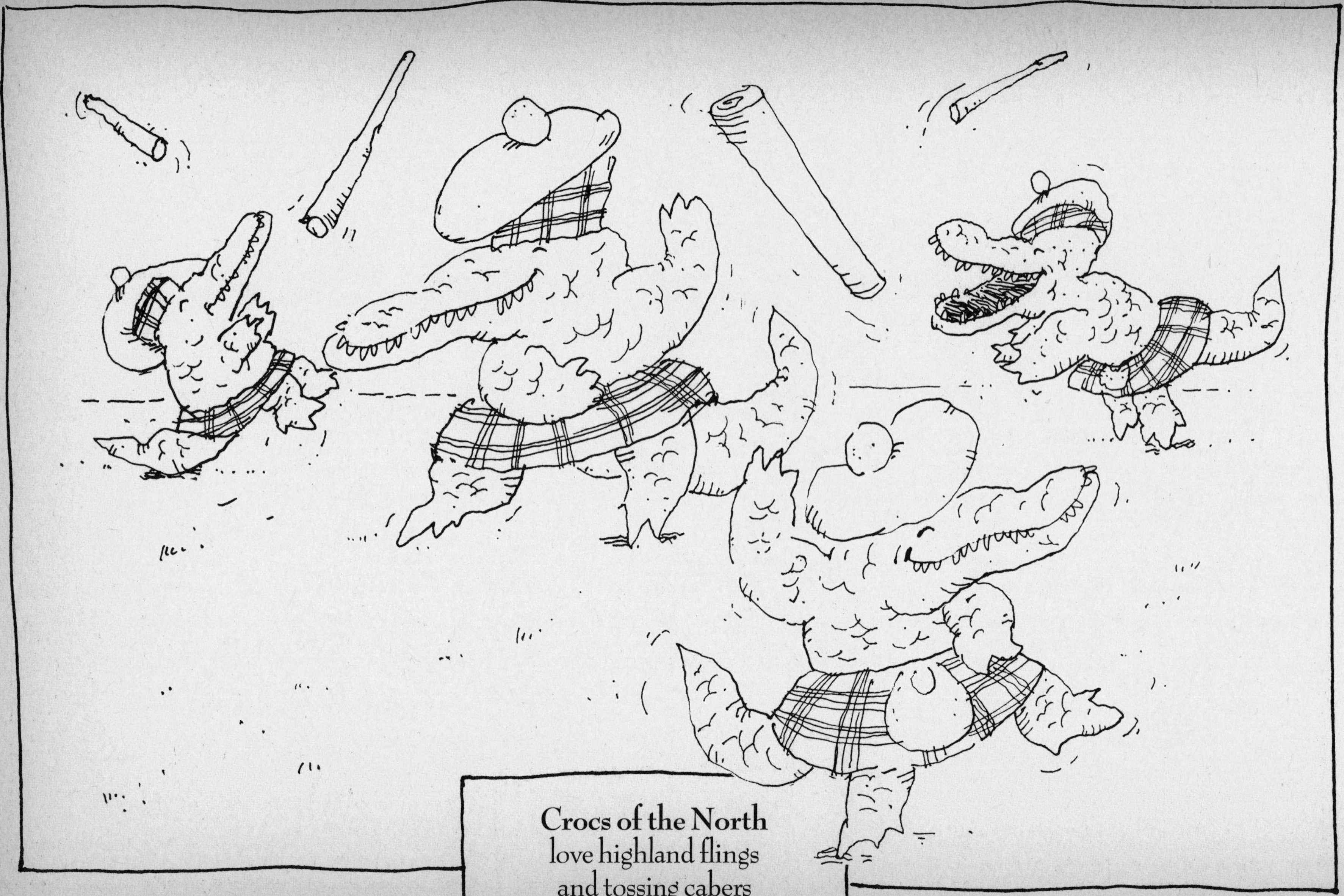

Crocs of the North
love highland flings
and tossing cabers
over things

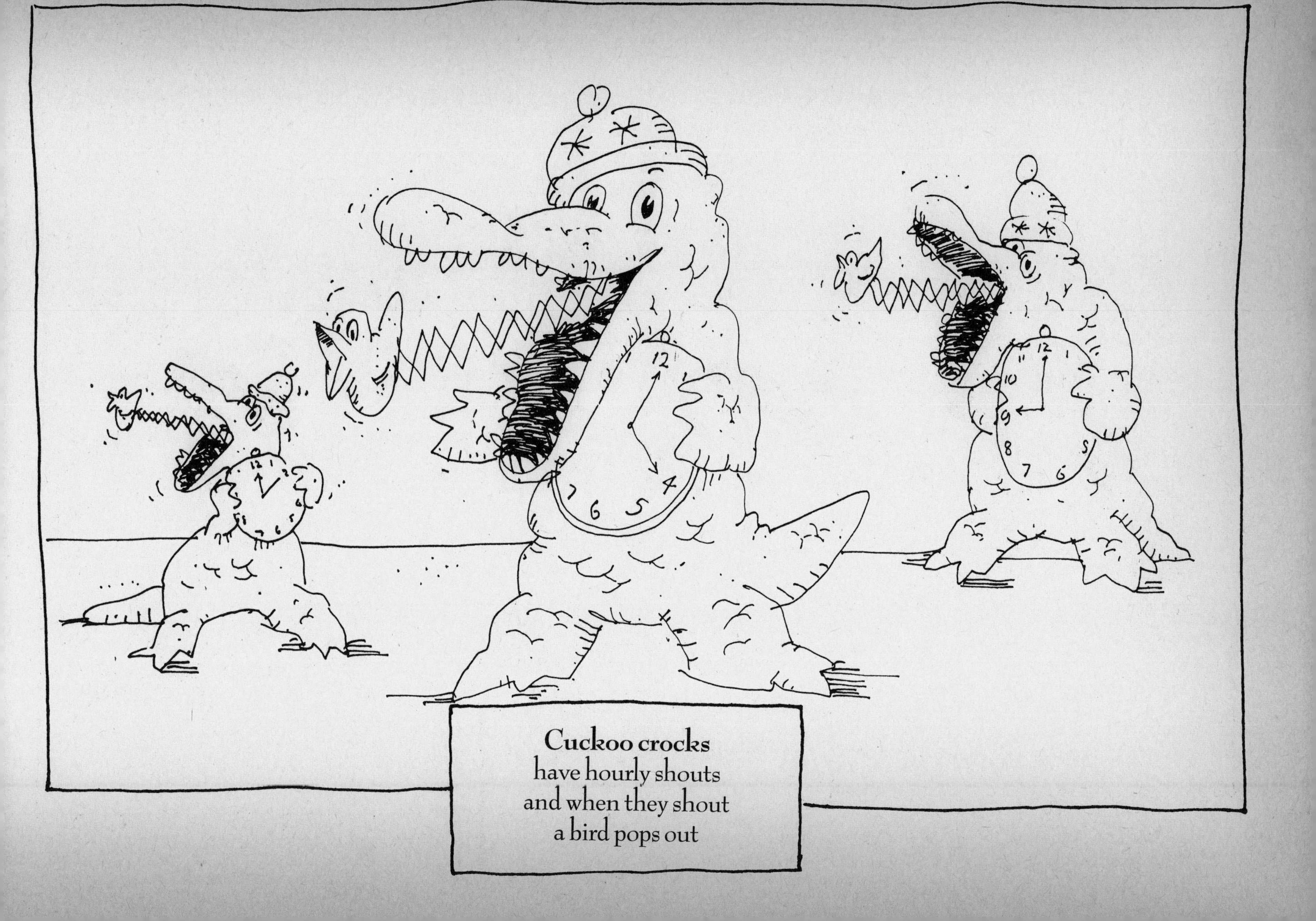

Cuckoo crocks
have hourly shouts
and when they shout
a bird pops out

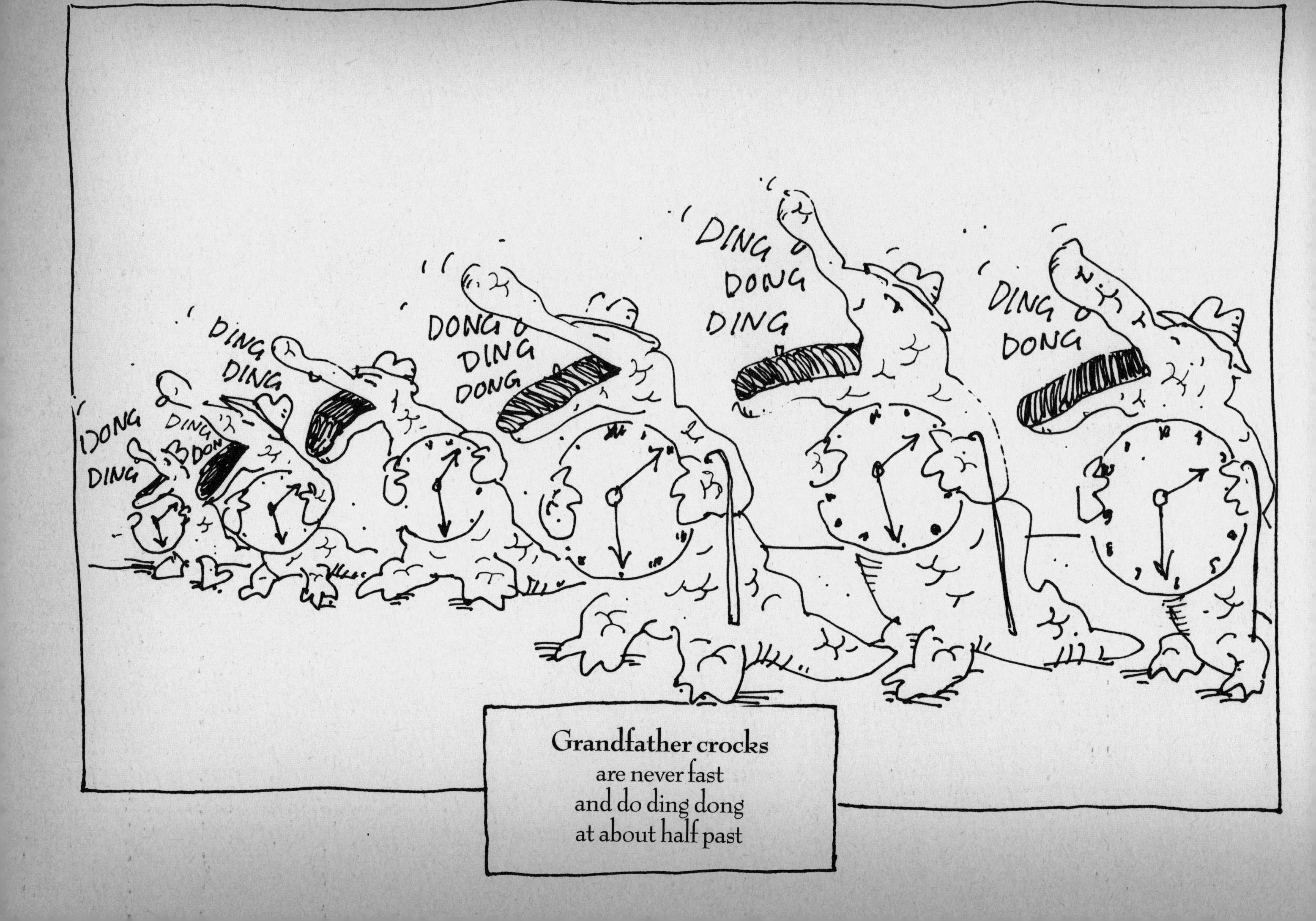
DONG DING
DING DON
DING DING
DONG DING DONG
DING DONG DING
DING DONG

Grandfather crocks
are never fast
and do ding dong
at about half past

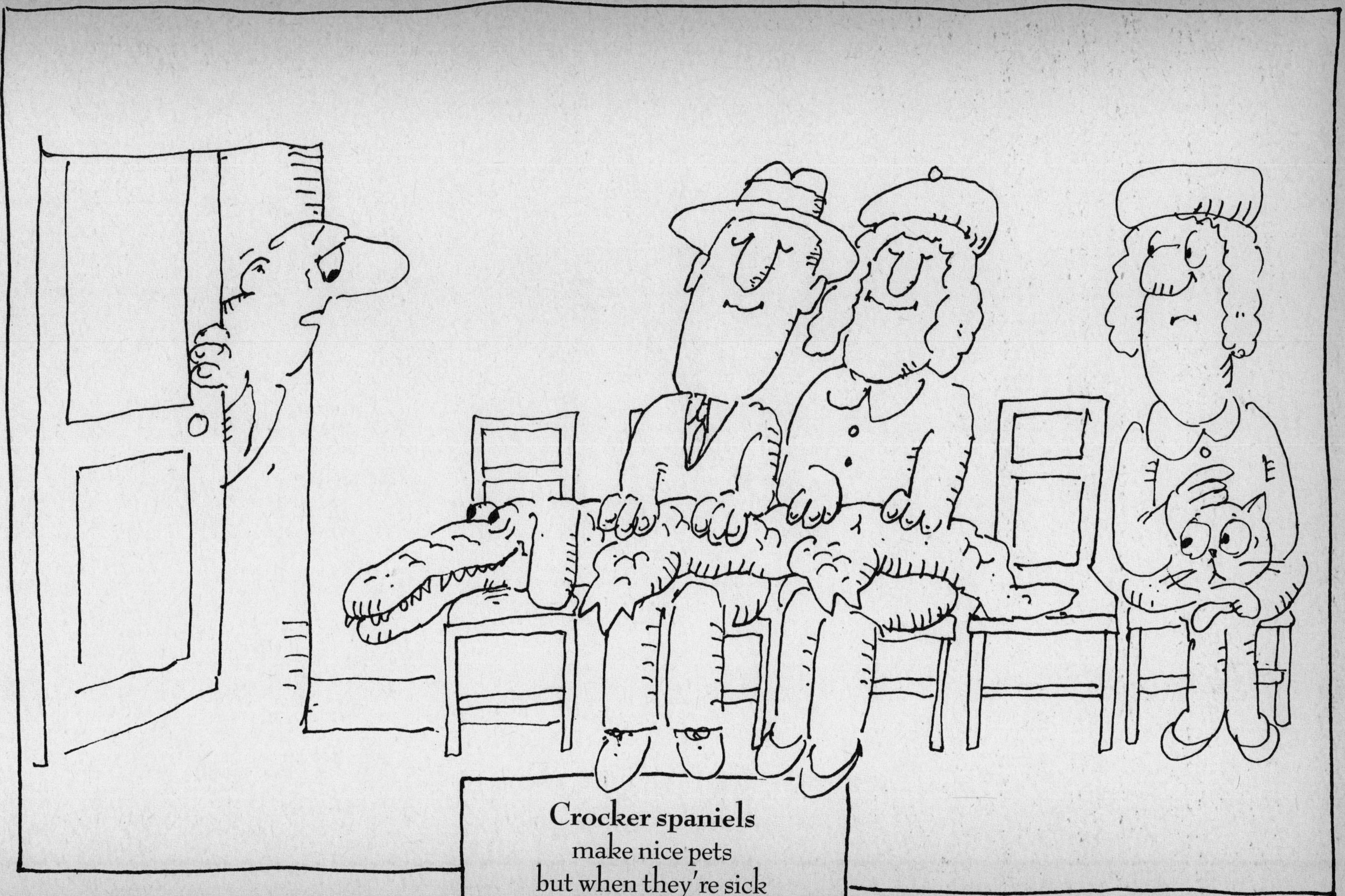

Crocker spaniels
make nice pets
but when they're sick
they upset vets

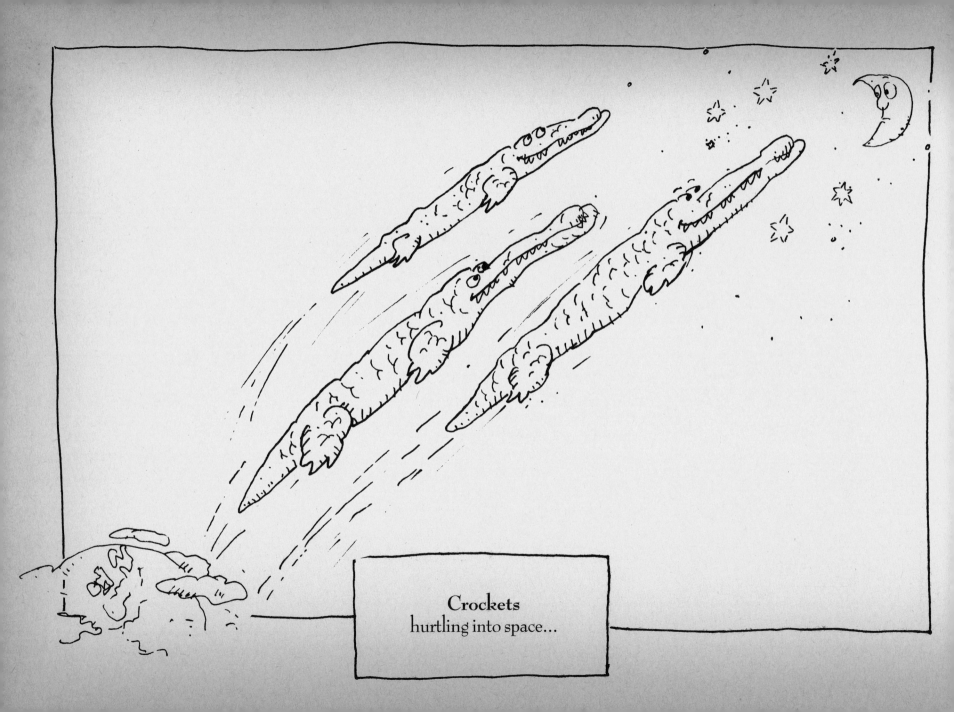

Crockets
hurtling into space...

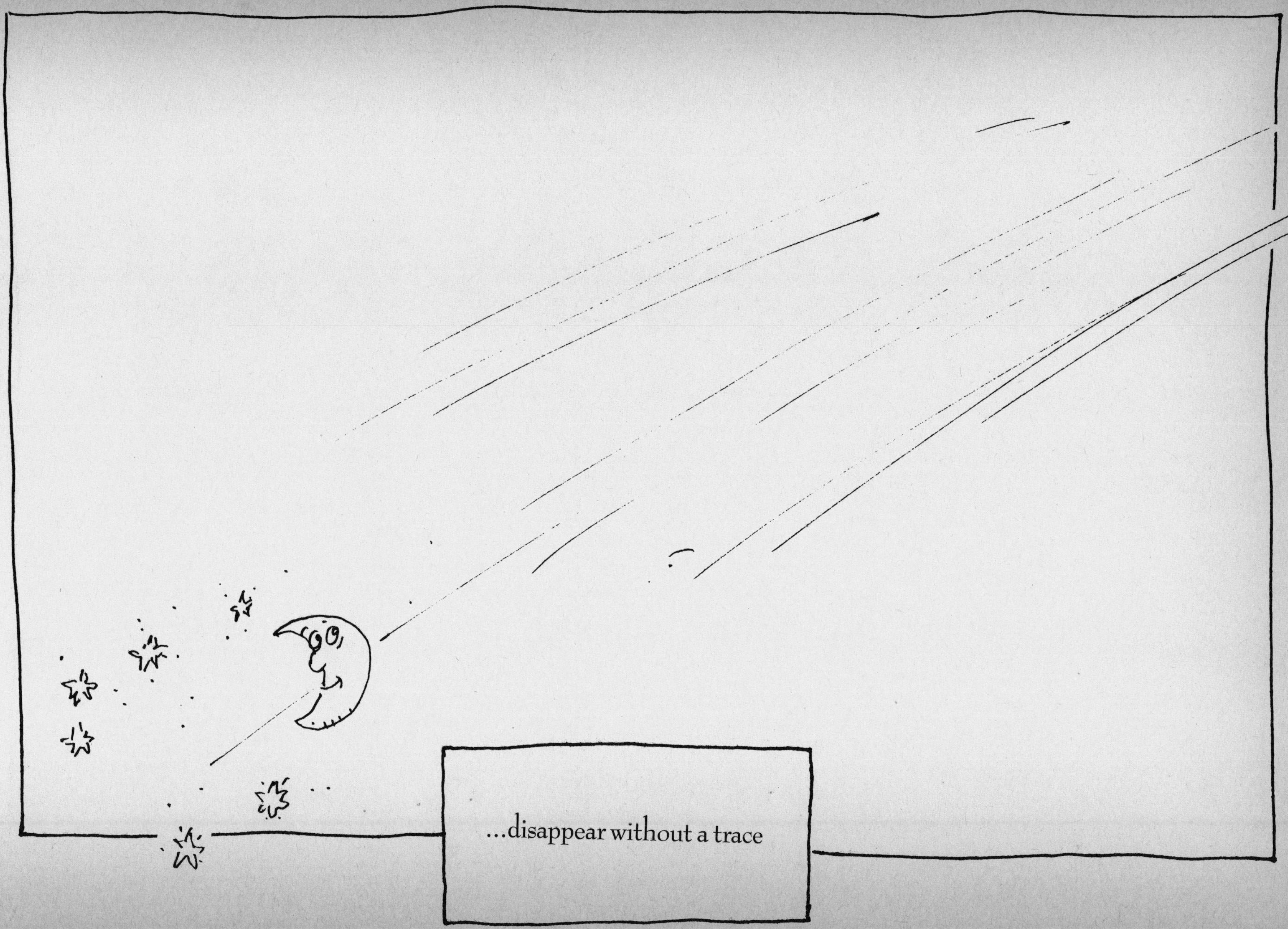
...disappear without a trace

...and croco-dulls
fill me with boredom
and that's the reason
I've ignored 'em